# THE ESSENTIAL GUIDE TO WICCA FOR BEGINNERS

# The Essential Guide to

# WICCA
## FOR BEGINNERS

## 52 Spells and Rituals
## Plus Magical History

AMYTHYST RAINE

ILLUSTRATIONS BY ALYSSA GONZALEZ

ROCKRIDGE
PRESS

For general information on our other products and services or to obtain technical support, please contact our Customer Care Department within the United States at (866) 744-2665, or outside the United States at (510) 253-0500.

Rockridge Press publishes its books in a variety of electronic and print formats. Some content that appears in print may not be available in electronic books, and vice versa.

Interior and Cover Designer: Karmen Lizzul
Art Producer: Samantha Ulban
Editor: Jesse Aylen
Production Editor: Emily Sheehan
Illustrations © 2020 Alyssa Gonzalez.

ISBN: Print 978-1-64739-814-9 | eBook 978-1-64739-489-9
R0

*This book is dedicated to my significant other, Roberto, for his support and encouragement through this writing process with humor, tenderness, and the ability to say the right thing at just the right time.*

# CONTENTS

# INTRODUCTION

Welcome to the beautiful world of Wicca, and congratulations on beginning your magical journey. If you've picked up this book, you must have felt the gentle tug that's going to lead you down a path of natural spirituality. Many people drawn to Wicca, who come from a variety of backgrounds and religions, say it is akin to "coming home." Wicca will lead you back to your roots and to the roots of a much older humankind.

My journey on this path began 46 years ago in the basement of my grandmother's house, where I cast my first spell with trembling hands and whispered incantations. I was seventeen, and the spell was about a boy, of course. With no Internet and no books on witchcraft to draw knowledge from, everything in those early days of my practice was done on a wing and a prayer.

Though my intention was immature, my energy scattered, and the outcome unpredictable, I realized then that witchcraft and magic are very real. I knew that I had much to learn and that if I were going to travel this spiritual path, it needed to be done with deep respect and moral integrity. Many years later, much to my astonishment, I discovered that my instincts had been right, the colors of my candles correct, and my basic spell structure on point—an innate natural knowing comes to some witches. It just might be the same for you!

I still embrace the path that I miraculously and instinctively stumbled upon so many years ago. It has been a rich spiritual journey with unimaginable connections to nature and the world around me, and a soulful connection to deities and energies unimagined. Witchcraft has led to a fulfilling and satisfying way of life, with a belief system that encourages individualism and responsible independence.

Practicing a spirituality outside the restrictive confines of more organized religions can be very liberating and exhilarating, but it carries with it a sense of spiritual responsibility. Practicing Wiccans take full responsibility for being in charge of their lives. They understand that they are accountable for their choices and actions and that those facets directly affect the people, the living things, and the earth around them.

Uniquely personal to each individual practitioner, the Wiccan path is built piece by piece, brick by brick, to form an extraordinary spiritual experience custom-made for the free-spirited witch. There is no right way or wrong way to practice witchcraft; there is only *your* way.

Wicca represents a lifetime of learning, experimenting, reading, and practicing, leading to amazing magical milestones. By opening this book, you've taken the first step toward spiritual enlightenment and a new path. Go forward in joy, anticipation, and wonder on this amazing journey, *your* amazing journey. Embrace the knowledge, the empathy, the compassion, and the spirit of the Wiccan.

# PART ONE

# Wiccan History, Beliefs, and Practices

What is Wicca? What are the origins of this unique spirituality? What do Wiccans believe, and how do they practice fantastic, mystical spell crafting and magic in the modern world? Soon you will become acquainted with the roots of Wicca, as well as the people who forged this path and whose fortitude and sacrifice paved the way for modern practitioners.

## CHAPTER 1

# Exploring the Roots of Wicca

Within this chapter, we'll discuss what constitutes the Wiccan spiritual path and how an individual can connect with its practices and beliefs. We'll also explore some of the colorful, inspirational, and founding characters who helped to birth this contemporary belief system.

# What Is Wicca?

Wicca is the spiritual path and practice of people commonly known as witches. Witchcraft is an ancient form of spirituality that closely mirrors earth-based shamanic practices of Indigenous people around the world. It encompasses the celebration of the seasons and agricultural milestones, recognizes the divine in both male and female deities, and embraces the natural life cycles of all living things.

The precursors of Wicca stretch back thousands of years to the British Isles and Europe, long before the dawn of Christianity, when spiritual practices centered on the seasonal cycles of nature. Early 20th-century practitioners rediscovered these celebrations and rituals and infused them with a healthy dose of nature worship. Today's Wicca embodies the free spirit of those nature-focused religions and embraces the original individualistic practices of the witch.

If you're confused, know that you're not alone; there is some confusion over the terms *Wiccan* and *witch*. These two terms have been used interchangeably in the modern world, and indeed, a Wiccan can be (and often is) a witch. However, there are Wiccans who do not consider themselves witches because they choose not to practice magic. They may follow many, or all, of the tenants of Wicca, but they don't use their power to harness natural energy and use it in accordance with their will, a practice that defines witchcraft.

On the other side of the coin, there are witches who do not consider themselves Wiccan. They cast spells, make magic, and often incorporate some of the spiritual practices of Wicca in their craft, but they don't embrace the entire Wiccan ideology.

Remember, there is no right or wrong way to practice witchcraft; there is only *your* way.

Wicca is a very gentle, balanced, and positive spirituality that wraps welcoming arms around the earth and all her creatures. It consists of nurturing practices centered around honoring the earth and protecting all living things through the working of magic, the celebration of the turning seasons, the recognition of divine power in both male and female deities, and the empowerment of discovering and honoring the positive energy within us all.

For many, Wicca is a way of life; it's who we are and how we live. It's how we grow, develop, and thrive. Wicca empowers the individual to be the best they can be and encourages growth, independence, and responsibility. Even more vitally, Wicca unleashes powerful energies that run through our world and ourselves and allows us to harness that energy to make magic happen.

A spiritual practice defined by the practitioner, Wicca can be a solitary path carved out through years of learning and practice or a structured group of coven practitioners who gather to celebrate, honor, and support each other.

## The Meaning of Magic

Magic is all about harnessing natural energy and being able to manipulate and move this energy to create positive changes. Wiccan magic differs from many non-Wiccan practices in the fact that there is a code of conduct associated with this spiritual path:

*Do what ye will, an' harm none.*

Wiccans believe that the energy and intentions you send out come back to you threefold, so you only want to send out positive energy and intentions for positive purposes.

Practicing magic means that you are taking responsibility for your life, your actions, and your actions' consequences and that you're capable of producing change where change is needed. Being a magic practitioner means that you have a responsibility to uphold the code of ethics embraced by many Wiccans and that you walk through this life, and on this path, without doing any harm.

Wicca differs from many mainstream religions in that the power of the divine is found within each and every one of us. When you cast spells, you

# Is Wicca Gendered?

Wiccan spirituality embraces the feminine divine, the Goddess, and female energy. Although Wicca recognizes both a male and female deity and is focused on finding balance with magical practice, witchcraft has long exemplified feminine power and the feminine mystique. For many, the word *witch* has been associated with *woman*.

During the growth and explosion of the women's movement in the 1970s, many women were heard to shout the mantra, "The goddess is alive, and magic is afoot!" True to that mantra, the patriarchal religions met their match when Wicca entered the scene with its beloved goddess and her wild, untamed spiritual energy. The culmination of this phenomenon was the development of Dianic Wicca, a spiritual path for women only, by Zsuzsanna Budapest.

Although witches have been traditionally thought of as female, Wicca is open to practitioners of all genders and expressions. An ever-evolving practice, Wicca mirrors the participants, the society, and the cultural changes around it. People of all genders have been stepping forward to claim not only their magical heritage, but the word *witch* as well.

Wicca is a synthesis of ancient practices rooted in mysticism and magic, as well as modern ideas of equality, inclusivity, and balance. This unique and amazingly individualistic spirituality is open to all who wish to embrace it with dedication, respect, and love.

are not requesting that divinity do something for you; you are taking control and creating change in conjunction with the natural spiritual energy that is part of you and part of the universe.

# The Quilt of Wiccan History

Today's practitioners owe the resurgence of paganism, Wicca, and witchcraft to innovative individuals who embraced and resurrected ancient practices to create a modern, relevant spirituality.

Wicca is a richly woven tapestry of pagan belief systems, divined and developed by individuals who were ahead of their time. These forebearers reconnected with the magic of ancient deities, nature-based reverence, a back-to-the-earth mentality, counterculture enthusiasm, and the independent spirit of the witch.

But no solitary individual is responsible for Wicca's rebirth and popularity; rather, we can thank a handful of farsighted, free-spirited people who chose to embrace the natural pull toward earth-based worship and the call of magic and witchcraft. These people, many of whom have become associated with modern paganism, emerged from cultures with their own rich history.

We will look first at neo-paganism and the individuals who forged the way for future generations, opening the door for others to connect with a natural spirituality and heritage. We will then look closer at the many branches of Wiccan belief.

## Wicca and Neo-Paganism

Neo-pagan religions are reconstructions of ancient pagan practices from Celtic, Greek, Roman, and Norse cultures, among others, that predate Christianity. Also known as contemporary paganism, neo-paganism often strives to reconstruct ancient paganism, embracing the deities and surviving traditions.

From a contemporary vantage point, neo-paganism reemerged to find global kinship with the cultural revolution of the 1960s. The energies of both movements involved honoring the earth, going back to basics, and protecting our resources and all living things. Neo-paganism was an epiphany: the concept of using magic to regain and retain personal power and the idea of divinity in the dual images of male and female interwoven with concepts of reincarnation, connection with Spirit, and an acceptance of personal experimentation.

Although the complete picture of magical practices from centuries ago, passed down by word of mouth, will always remain somewhat of an enigma, enough knowledge survived time and repression for the modern Wiccan to proudly and confidently reclaim this heritage.

## A Wiccan by Any Other Name

Wicca is a term that envelops a variety of spiritual paths and practices, some overlapping within traditions, and others unique within an individualistic belief system. There are several Wiccan traditions, much like there are different denominations within Christianity or Judaism. Some of these traditions embrace the structure of a coven and the hierarchy within it to include specific studies rewarded by initiation. Some embrace the Wiccan Rede to "harm none," and others carry very specific codes of conduct and expectation for members. There are Wiccan paths that celebrate the traditional esbats and sabbats, and there are those that focus more on political activism and awareness. Together, we'll explore their unique histories and facets.

### GARDNERIAN WICCA

Gardnerian Wicca was developed in the 1950s by Gerald Gardner, a British civil servant and amateur scholar of paganism and magic. Gardner developed his Wiccan path from some of the beliefs and practices of the New

Forest coven, into which he was initiated in 1939. Gardner's Wiccan path is considered British Traditional Wicca, and many later forms of Wicca sprang from those individuals originally initiated into the coven Gardner founded, called the Bricket Wood coven, as an offshoot of the original New Forest coven.

## ALEXANDRIAN WICCA

Alexandrian Wicca was developed by Alex Sanders, often referred to as "King of the Witches," along with his wife, Maxine Sanders, in the 1960s. Sanders's Wiccan path is very similar to Gardnerian Wicca, in which he was trained, but it adds practices of the Kabbalah. Although Alexandrian Wicca is more eclectic than the Gardnerian tradition, it does follow a series of levels of study and initiations for its members. Sanders believed strongly in coven initiation and lineage, and his motto was "It takes a witch to make a witch." The Sanders are also associated with the saying "If it works, use it."

## ALGARD WICCA

The Algard tradition was created in 1972 by Mary Nesnick, an initiate of both the Gardnerian and Alexandrian traditions. Because of this fusion, Nesnick's Wiccan path is considered British Traditional Wicca.

## SEAX WICCA

The Seax tradition was founded in 1973 by Raymond Buckland, a British-born initiate of the Gardnerian tradition who moved to Ohio. Buckland's tradition highlights the celebration of Woden, Thunor, Freya, and Twi, representing the horned god and the mother goddess. His books on witchcraft embrace both the experienced witch and the newcomer, providing enough instruction for the beginner to self-initiate and consecrate their first tools.

Buckland's Wiccan tradition has a very democratic energy, as Seax practitioners elect their high priest and priestess from within the coven. Minimal ceremonial tools are used; instead, they embrace the use of runes and encourage self-initiation.

## CELTIC WICCA

Seen as a form of both Wicca and Celtic neo-paganism, Celtic Wicca incorporates the deities of Celtic mythology and the celebration of seasonal milestones in its tradition. Celtic Wicca has been criticized for cultural appropriation because it embraces the fantasy and mysticism of Celtic myths and legends rather than more historically accurate points. However, Celtic Wicca is beloved and embraced as a form of spirituality by its followers.

There are other variations of the very popular Celtic Wiccan traditions, which include American Celtic Wicca, created by Lady Sheba (Jessie Bell), and Celtic Wicca, created by Gavin and Yvonne Frost, which is a loosely combined spiritual practice consisting of some general Wiccan practices and a big dose of Celtic mythology.

## DIANIC WICCA

Founded in the 1970s by Zsuzsanna Budapest, Dianic Wicca differs from other Wiccan traditions in that only the Goddess is recognized and celebrated. Womanhood, folk practices, and healing magic are the center point of Dianic Wicca, along with the celebration of women's mysteries. A predominantly female-influenced spirituality, it has provoked controversy for its founder's insistence that only cisgender women (which she calls "born women") be granted coven membership.

Dianic Wiccans worship the Goddess through her myriad identities within all cultures but have a special affinity for Artemis. The rituals of this Wiccan tradition include meditation, visualization, spell work, and healing modern womanhood from the injuries and injustice of the patriarchy. They create covens that are loosely structured and nonhierarchical, and they celebrate the esbats and Wiccan holidays.

## RECLAIMING WICCA

Launched with a class in 1980 taught by Starhawk and Diane Baker in the San Francisco Bay Area, Reclaiming Wicca is reminiscent of the 1960s with its cultural and political awareness. Most notably, there is a lack of hierarchy in this Wiccan tradition, with no high priest or priestess, no specific rituals or pantheons, and no traditional initiation.

The motto of Reclaiming Wicca is "Speak as the Spirit moves you."
Self-improvement, creativity, self-discovery, and self-empowerment are all encouraged. Political activism has been a fundamental part of Reclaiming Wicca, as well as the discouragement of using any type of drugs for meditation or energy building. "Witch camps" across the country train and teach up-and-coming practitioners about witchcraft.

## Wicca Goes Underground

In 1486, one of the most notorious books ever written, *Malleus Malefi-carum* by Heinrich Kramer, appeared, sparking the race to exterminate anyone suspected of practicing witchcraft. Kramer's tome, often trans-lated to "The Witch's Hammer," was used as a guideline for identifying suspected witches and gathering evidence to condemn them to death. This manual was used in Europe during the time of the Inquisition to exe-cute suspected witches—mostly women, and many of them elder women.

# Wiccans in History

In this section, we will look at some of the most impressive and memorable figures who contributed to the revival of witchcraft and the creation of Wicca in the 20th century.

### Dr. Margaret Murray (1863–1963)

Dr. Murray was a British anthropologist who believed that the witch trials were an attempt to eradicate a surviving pagan religion that predated Christianity and worshiped a male god and a female goddess. She was involved in the early feminist movement and is the author of *The Witch-Cult in Western Europe* (1921) and *The God of the Witches* (1931).

### Aleister Crowley (1875–1947)

Crowley was the bad boy of the pagan world. He was a ceremonial magician, an occultist, and the founder of an offshoot path called Thelema. He gained notoriety for experimental drug use, as well as other hedonistic and sexual appetites. His motto was "Do what thou will," and he certainly did. Crowley is the author of *Liber AL vel Legis*, commonly known as *The Book of the Law* (1904).

### Gerald Gardner (1884–1964)

An instrumental figure in bringing Wicca into the contemporary world and allowing it to take its place as a genuine religion, Gardner is known as "The Father of Wicca" and creator of the Gardnerian tradition. He was the director of the Museum of Magic and Witchcraft on the Isle of Man until his death. He is the author of *Witchcraft Today* (1954) and *The Meaning of Witchcraft* (1959).

### Raymond Buckland (1934–2017)

Buckland was a British occultist and Wiccan initiated in the Gardnerian tradition, as well as the creator of the Seax Wiccan tradition. After moving to the United States in 1962, he opened the first museum of witchcraft and magic in the country. Buckland allegedly claimed to be the first person in the United States to openly admit to being Wiccan. He is the author of *Buckland's Complete Book of Witchcraft* (1986), which is often referred to as "The Big Blue Book" and is considered a classic.

### Scott Cunningham (1956–1993)

A prolific pagan author, Cunningham wrote numerous titles, some which are considered classic, including *Cunningham's Encyclopedia of Magical Herbs* (1985) and *Cunningham's Encyclopedia of Crystal, Gem, and Metal Magic* (1988). He began as an initiate in a coven in 1982 but soon left the group. The epitome of the solitary practitioner, he believed that Wicca should be a less closed tradition and more open to newcomers, and many of his books reflect and encourage this idea.

From February 1692 to May 1693, this horror came to what is now Massachusetts with the Salem witch trials. The first person accused of witchcraft was Tituba, an enslaved woman denounced by two teenage girls, Elizabeth Parris and Abigail Williams. With that levied accusation, the stage was set for the en masse accusation of more than 200 people of being practicing witches. In retrospect, this is considered one of the worst recorded cases of mass hysteria.

From what would come to be called "the burning times," there arose in the 1900s a legion of far-seeing, inventive, creative, spiritual, and magical people. These brave souls, and their fearless persistence to embrace their unique individualism and spirituality, would set the stage for the rest of us to step out of the shadows and into the light. The 20th century would see an impressive resurrection of witchcraft leading to the birth of Wicca.

## The Contemporary Wiccan

Long gone are the days people accused of witchcraft can be arrested, tortured into a confession, and executed in Europe or the United States. It should be noted, though, that the last arrest for the practice of witchcraft in the UK didn't take place until 1941, at the height of World War II, with the British military fearing that the spiritual contact a woman named Helen Duncan had with a dead soldier would compromise security. The British Witchcraft Act of 1735, making witchcraft and its practice illegal, was not formally repealed until 1951.

As progressive and accepting as parts of the world may be toward witchcraft and paganism, there are still places where it may not be safe to openly practice witchcraft or flaunt or espouse pagan beliefs. Areas of the Middle East and Africa are not open to the idea of witchcraft, and practitioners can face dire consequences if accused.

In this modern age, it's generally recognized that witches are not evil but are in fact often healers and caretakers of the earth, seers, magic makers, or herbalists, living their lives like everyone else, striving to make wise choices while embracing a uniquely fulfilling spiritual practice.

The 21st century has seen extraordinary advances in the acceptance of Wicca as a religion deserving of acknowledgment and respect. Though some people still prefer to keep their Wiccan practice private, there are many more who have come out of the broom closet, so to speak, openly practicing and actively contradicting prejudices in the process.

Wicca has helped contemporary practitioners connect with a spirituality that honors the individual, reconnects us with nature in an intimately healing way, and makes us more aware of the wider web of energy running through all living things. Many who have discovered Wicca have found a spiritual balance otherwise difficult to imagine, one that soothes the soul in a magical way.

The modern world has redefined coven practice with connections made through the Internet. It's easier now to find and interact with like-minded individuals, to practice our spirituality together, to share knowledge and learn, and to grow in understanding. At the opposite end of the spectrum, the modern world has delightfully unleashed the knowledge and information a solitary practitioner needs in order to forge their own unique path, through informative websites, blogs, and books that open the door to infinite possibilities.

# In Summary

Now that we've had a look at the origins of witchcraft, what it's overcome, and the individuals who had a hand in shaping and birthing what we know today as Wicca, it's time to broaden our knowledge with a look at the beliefs and practices associated with the craft. It's time to come another step closer to the Wiccan path.

## CHAPTER 2

# Wiccan Beliefs and Practices

We will look at the key beliefs and practices of daily Wiccan life. We'll explore deities and how we connect with them; how we interact with the natural world, including the earth, the celestial bodies, and the elements; and how it all comes together with transitional and seasonal celebrations during the year.

# Before You Practice

As you decide how you will approach your newfound spiritual path, you'll want to consider whether you'll make this journey a solitary one or whether you'll welcome and benefit from the camaraderie of a coven. Always remember, this is *your* spiritual path. These decisions are yours, and yours alone, to make.

## Meeting the Wiccan Within

Wicca can be an extraordinarily personal spiritual journey and experience. It may be different for every practitioner. A Wiccan will travel a unique road that leads to a deeper connection with nature, and through their commitment, they can experience an understanding and acceptance of natural transitions, along with a wonderous sense of self-empowerment. The Wiccan becomes one with Spirit, the divine; is connected to earth, the mother; and has a deep soul connection to the energies of the universe that help them maneuver through mortal existence with renewed purpose, strength, and direction.

But how do you discover this path?

For many people, there is an innate "knowing" that there is something unusual about themselves, but they often can't quite put their finger on exactly what it is. At some point in life, they will have an epiphany, something that will shine a light on the bigger picture. Other people will feel drawn by their natural connection to divination, herbs, crystals and stones, or their unique spiritual gifts. Still others will delve into an interest in pagan deities with a curiosity about magic and other esoteric topics, driven by a feeling that there's more out there than what society has to offer.

For those of you who prefer being by yourselves and pursuing solitary endeavors, a solitary practice may be to your liking. You'll study and learn on your own, at your own pace and guided by your innate curiosities. You'll gather tools and experience along with knowledge, and when the time feels right, you will self-initiate into the world of Wicca and in the tradition you choose (should you choose one).

Others who feel the calling may have the urge to connect with a group, a coven, for instruction and fellowship with like-minded individuals. Some may wish to begin a course of formal study and follow the degree system within an organized group. (We'll take a closer look at coven initiation and magical practice in chapter 4.)

Whatever way you choose to travel on this spiritual journey, the direction you take and the roads you build will be unique to you. You'll discover that just as we go through various phases at different ages and stages of life, so will your spiritual journey. The world is not set in stone but is fluid and changeable. The evolution of your Wiccan practice will also be fluid, shaping itself to adapt to you as you progress on this path.

## Awakening the Wiccan Within

The call to any spirituality is unique and special to each individual. Signs you may pick up that will lead you in the direction of Wicca can be varied—some subtle and others louder and more direct.

For some of us, the invitation to follow the Wiccan path comes in the form of spirit animals, totems, and forms showing up repeatedly in our lives, making us aware. For example, the raven sitting on your front porch at dawn may suddenly show up in sculpture and paintings at unexpected moments, only to reappear in your dreams at night. For others it could be a phrase showing up in the lyrics of a song, printed on a billboard for us to see as we pass by, and spoken unexpectedly by a stranger. Or perhaps it's the natural magnetism we feel to organics, plants, and herbs and the strong desire to learn about and use them, or a special affinity for and connection to the turning seasons and other subtle signs from the earth.

Perhaps you are one of those born with natural gifts like second sight, particularly strong and unusual empathy, or the ability to turn life's events in your direction with powerful thoughts and subliminal suggestions.

Whatever it is that triggers an awareness of Wicca within you, it has reached you. You are awakened to the calling and answering it, because you are here.

# Understanding Wiccan Deities and Values

At the core of the Wiccan philosophy is the Wiccan Rede "An' it harm none, do what thou will." (See page 38 for more on this.) As maligned and misunderstood as real witchcraft has been through the centuries, it honors and respects all life.

There is a unique balance in Wicca of male and female energy; both are sacred and divine. Wicca honors the Goddess, women, and women's mysteries with reverence and respect, but there is also a wider array of sacred figures and energy to explore.

## The Goddess

The Goddess is connected to the moon, the phases of which mirror the three faces of the Goddess: the Maiden, the Mother, and the Crone. The Goddess and her faces in turn mirror a woman's life stages.

### THE MAIDEN

The Maiden is represented by the crescent moon. She is new beginnings. She is hope and a sweet naiveté that comes from inexperience and great doses of optimism defined by an untainted spirit. She is woman at the threshold of life, with choices and directions yet to be made and determined. She is unbridled youth, with dreams to dream and wishes to fulfill.

### THE MOTHER

The Mother is represented by the full moon. She is existence at its most fertile, whether it's fertility of body, mind, or spirit. She is woman at her most creative, filled with ideas and dreams to bring to fruition. The Mother is the nurturer, whether of children, dreams, men, or the earth itself. She is the hub of the wheel of life, with a universe of spokes radiating from her center.

## THE CRONE

The Crone is represented by the dark moon. She is experience, knowledge, and wisdom sought out by multitudes. She stands at heights that allow her to view both the past and the future at the same time. She is the woman who has brought to fruition the maiden's dreams, and now she is able to look back upon a life well lived and well learned. She stands equally at the threshold of the end and a new beginning.

# The God

The God is connected to the sun, whose energy and radiance warm our existence, lighting the way with healing for the body, mind, and spirit. The three faces of the God relate to man and his journey through life as he passes various stages: the Green Man, the Horned God, and the Sage.

## THE GREEN MAN

The Green Man represents new growth and great promise. His energy is associated with spring and rebirth, the new growth of foliage, and movement toward fertility and the promise of harvest. He is the young man beginning his journey, full of enthusiasm and the will to succeed, inexperienced and optimistic, and eagerly stepping forward to start life.

## THE HORNED GOD

The Horned God symbolizes fertility, virility, and strength. His energy is centered around reproduction and sex. This god represents man in the middle of life, fertile with ideas set to action and full of movement and unbridled energy. His feet are firmly planted in determination, strength, and courage. He brings to fruition that which was at first only imagined.

## THE SAGE

The Sage is the god of wisdom, a wise teacher full of experience. This is the man who has lived life and met the expectations of his role. He is the mentor for a younger generation coming behind him. He is the example to younger men just awakening to life and its myriad possibilities. The Sage will have the answers that many seek.

## The Earthly and the Celestial

The celestial bodies of the sky carry energy and magic. This has been tracked through the intricacies of astrology, as well as through the manipulation of their celestial energy during magical rituals and spells. Together, let's look at the sun, the moon, and individual planets and their places within the Wiccan tradition.

### THE SUN

The sun is filled with male energy of the God. Invoke its power for men's issues, for their health, healing, and general well-being. Trauma and relationship issues benefit from this in-your-face potent energy. The sun will force you to look at issues you've been avoiding, and it will provide you with the energy needed to find solutions.

CORRESPONDENCES
Day: **Sunday**
Colors: **orange, yellow, gold**
Herbs: **marigold, St. John's wort, sunflower, eyebright**
Stones: **amber, yellow topaz, diamond**

### THE MOON

The moon has many faces, from waxing to waning, to dark and gibbous, and each carries its own special resonance when you're casting spells and working your magic.

**Waxing Moon:** It's all about magic that will bring something to you, working toward the fruition of a spell. Use the waxing moon like a magnet to draw to you your heart's desires.

**Waning Moon:** You will be sending something away from you, banishing it with the energy of the waning moon. As it shrinks and goes away, so will the thing you want to be rid of.

 **The Dark Moon:** As the moon grows dark and disappears in the night sky, it touches the deepest, most mysterious part of us, where our intuition dwells. The dark moon is the time for divination.

 **The Gibbous Moons:** These are the midway points. The waxing gibbous is used when there is something you need to draw to you. The waning gibbous will be used when something needs to be gone. Spells cast on the gibbous moons manifest either at the full or dark moon, depending upon which specific gibbous energy you're using.

## CORRESPONDENCES
Day: **Monday**
Colors: **blue, gray, silver**
Herbs: **calamus, jasmine, myrrh, sandalwood**
Stones: **moonstone, pearl, aquamarine**

## THE PLANETS

The energy of heavenly bodies is used in magical practice, with each planet's energy affecting very specific areas of life. Just as the planets are interwoven with astrology, influencing our personalities and psyches, they equally have the ability to move energy through spell casting for a plethora of intentions, enriching our magical lives and our enchantments in turn.

 **Mercury** is perfect for issues of communication and creativity. Mercury energy moves fast, so this heavenly body can be used to speed up a process. It encompasses the lucidity of pure thought and imagination.

**Venus** is ideal for magic dealing with love and romance, emotions, and self-confidence, as in beauty and self-improvement spells.

 **Earth** energy is all about physical manifestation. It's necessary for spells of health and healing. The magic of Earth encompasses what you can see, touch, taste, hear, and smell.

 **Mars** is the epitome of strength, filled with the valor and courage of the warrior. It helps us deal with tough issues for which resolve and determination are needed.

 **Jupiter** is all about expansion and making things grow, and this energy is especially attuned to finances, business, and legal issues.

 **Saturn** is a somewhat darker, more intense energy that is useful for spells of protection and legal issues, as well as magic for justice.

 **Uranus** is all about eccentricity and individualism. This planet's energy is perfect for spells that will unleash and enhance these qualities.

 **Neptune** with its dreamy water traits lends itself to energy diffused with idealism, imagination, and fantasy. When spell casting, consider Neptune your fairy godmother.

# The Four Elements and the Spirit

The four elements and the power of Spirit propel the Wiccan forward with energy to manifest magical spells. They are at the core of belief in the natural world's power and energy and the inherent energy that comes from within the Wiccan, and they are vital to life itself.

### FIRE

Fire is passion that burns from the core of our being. This is the energy that drives us forward and inflames our will and courage to succeed. It's the energy that drives lovers together against all odds and that fights tirelessly for justice.

Use fire for spells of transition, to clear out or burn off the chaff of life. The element of fire is profoundly connected to candle magic. Allow the flame to consume spell papers, herbs, or other items connected to your intention, and toss the ashes to the wind.

See the table on page 26 for some correspondences to help your magic align with the powerful, passionate element of fire.

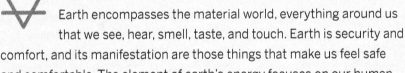

### EARTH

Earth encompasses the material world, everything around us that we see, hear, smell, taste, and touch. Earth is security and comfort, and its manifestation are those things that make us feel safe and comfortable. The element of earth's energy focuses on our human appetites, those things of a material nature that make our life comfortable and enjoyable.

Incorporate the element of earth into your spells through the use of salt, by the symbol of the pentacle, and by burying the remnants of a spell (candle wax, herbs, or other objects) in the ground.

See the table on page 26 for some correspondences to help you connect with the element of earth to ground yourself and your magical work.

| | | ELEMENT | | | |
|---|---|---|---|---|---|
| | | **FIRE** | **EARTH** | **AIR** | **WATER** | **SPIRIT** |
| **C O R R E S P O N D E N C E S** | **DIRECTION** | South | North | East | West | all directions |
| | **ENERGY** | masculine | feminine | masculine | feminine | masculine and feminine |
| | **COLOR** | red | green | yellow | blue | white |
| | **ELEMENTAL** | salamanders | gnomes | fairies | undines | angels |
| | **SEASON** | summer | winter | spring | autumn | all seasons |
| | **HERMETIC AXIOM** | "to dare" | "to know" | "to will" | "to keep silent" | |
| | **ZODIAC** | Aries, Leo, Sagittarius | Taurus, Virgo, Capricorn | Libra, Gemini, Aquarius | Cancer, Scorpio, Pisces | all signs |

## AIR

Air is our very breath and the voice we speak with. It carries the spark of creativity. Air moves us through time with communication, enabling the creation of words, music, and art. Air embraces the Wiccan's power to create something from nothing.

Incorporate the element of air into your spells with the use of incense, feathers, and music, as well as by using the wind to move energy and intentions through the universe. For instance, hang spell papers or spell bags on a tree limb and allow the breeze to carry the energy along.

You'll find that the correspondences in the table on page 26 will aid you in your connection with the element of air and the mental aspect of magic.

## WATER

Water is dreams, visions, and almost-imperceptible voices sent to us by the angels, our spirit animals, and totems. Water is divination and mysticism, an unquenchable thirst for knowing the unknown and seeing the unseen. Water is the mystery that lies in the Wiccan's soul.

Incorporate the element of water in your spells by cleansing certain tools, as well as your rocks and crystals, beneath running water. Create dream bags with blue stones to place in your pillowcase, and use morning dew for spells of beauty.

Use the correspondences in the table on page 26 to incorporate the magic of water into your spells to enhance divination and connect with your psychic center.

## SPIRIT

Spirit is the divine, no matter what you call it or how you find it. It is the breath of life, the savior, the power that moves the universe, and male energy and female energy. Spirit is unique and personal for everyone.

Of all the magical elements, Spirit is the most open-ended with its correspondences. You invite it into your circle and work with it through your magic itself.

# The Freedom of Belief

As you progress on your Wiccan journey, be open to possibilities beyond the boundaries of the familiar and the mundane. Take advantage of the freedom you have within the Wiccan world to explore the pantheons and connect with deities that resonate with you and your core beliefs and desires.

As you begin, ask yourself the following questions: How do you relate to the elements, seasons, holidays, and magic? What's important for you to connect with on this spiritual frontier? What is unique to you and your needs? What do you thirst to know more about on a deeply meaningful level? As a newcomer to this path, don't be hesitant to explore possibilities that you may discover unexpectedly while you read, learn, and grow. Embrace your individual gifts, and don't be afraid to try new things.

One of the most empowering options about this spirituality is the personal choices you can make to build your path and your practice one step at a time. Find out how you connect with Spirit and magic within the Wiccan world, for this connection will be uniquely your own.

And always enjoy the journey.

# The Wiccan's Year

Wiccans are keenly attuned to the organic cycles of nature, particularly the turning of the seasons and the changes that accompany them across a range of climates. There is a natural ebb and flow to time, and to the earth's rotation, that weave a vital bond with the Wiccan. As you'll learn, these points in time are celebrated with an ongoing spirit of joy, reverence, and anticipation.

The Gregorian calendar holds little significance to the Wiccan. The months no longer align to the full moons; the number of the years is insignificant to pagans, as they simply count the number of years since the birth of Christ; and the names of the months themselves have little to no significant meanings.

Here, we're going to explore the *Wiccan* year, the pivotal points of pagan celebration, and how the natural flow of time and the changing of the seasons can be observed from your magical viewpoint. As you celebrate the pagan holidays along the Wheel of the Year, you will reconnect with nature and its natural cycles, gain an understanding of our pagan roots and how these celebrations play into mainstream religions today, and build a special bond and relationship to Spirit with your dedicated practice.

By deepening and committing yourself to these observances, you will become familiar with the uniquely powerful energies of each full moon and the hidden magic and potential in this energy, as well as within yourself.

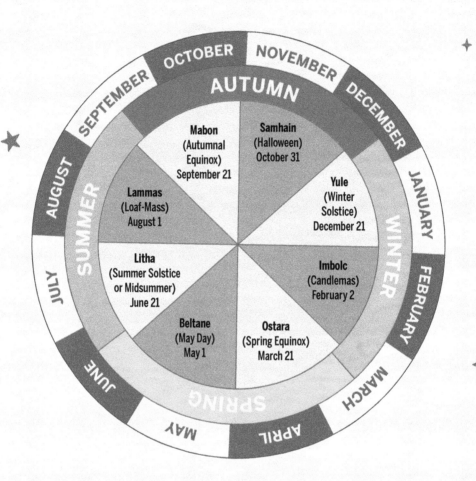

## The Wheel of the Year

The Wheel of the Year signifies traveling through the seasons and marking pagan holidays for celebration. Many Christian holidays familiar in mainstream society actually began as pagan holidays that were simply incorporated into the new Christian faith and calendar, as many were beloved and entrenched in memory and traditions.

Don't be surprised when you discover that some of the holidays, as well as the ways they're celebrated, seem familiar, including colored eggs, yule logs, and maypoles.

# The Sabbats

From Yule to Samhain, prepare to rejoice and celebrate your Wiccan faith.

## YULE (WINTER SOLSTICE)

**December 21**

This is a celebration acknowledging the longest day of darkness and welcoming the return of the sun. The legendary myth for Yule includes the battle between brothers, the Holly King and the Oak King. The Oak King will be victorious at Yule, and the growing season will return to the world. As part of the celebration, it's traditional to burn a Yule log and to decorate the house with pine cones, holly, and mistletoe.

## IMBOLC (CANDLEMAS)

**February 2**

Imbolc is a celebration of the goddess Brigid, the young maiden of spring, and an acknowledgment of the return of fertility to the world. As we honor Brigid, it's customary to cast healing spells and perform cleansing rituals and house blessings. Candle magic is especially powerful at this time, and this is also a popular time for initiations.

## OSTARA (SPRING EQUINOX)

**March 21**

This is a celebration of the Saxon goddess Ostara, as well as an acknowledgment of the return of fertility and the growing season. Ostara is deeply linked to ancient agricultural roots, celebrating the fertility of farm animals with colored eggs and images of rabbits. It's a time for planting and sowing, spells of rejuvenation, and spring cleaning.

## BELTANE (MAY DAY)

### May 1

This celebration of fertility and sexuality recognizes and honors human sexual expression. Beltane has an especially pagan flair. It's customary to dance around a maypole (a phallic symbol), weaving together brightly colored streamers (symbolic of the creative force of sex).

## LITHA (SUMMER SOLSTICE OR MIDSUMMER)

### June 21

A celebration of the longest day in the year, this holiday is also an acknowl-edgment of the growing season, as the harvest is soon to come. There is magic in the air at midsummer, and it's customary to gather herbs on this day, to revel in sun magic and spells, and to bless your familiar. This is also a time for dream work. All-night fairy vigils are always a fun way to observe the holiday, whether or not the fairies cooperate.

## LAMMAS (LOAF-MASS)

### August 1

Bread is a highlight of Lammas festivities, which celebrate the first harvest of the year: wheat. Magic for prosperity and purification is popular, as are rituals filled with wonderful baked goods using wheat and thanking the earth for its bounty.

## MABON (AUTUMNAL EQUINOX)

### September 21

The celebration of Mabon acknowledges an end of the year's growing season and a return to the approaching darker months. Popular at this time are spells for protection from the coming winter, harmony spells, harvest moon rituals, and past-life work. An ancient pagan festival with the burning a large wicker human form is traditional. It's generally filled with vegetation and is a somber acknowledgment of the end of harvest.

## SAMHAIN (HALLOWEEN)

October 31

At a time when the veil between the world of the living and the dead is thinnest, this solemn celebration honors ancestors and family members who have passed. At Samhain, some pagan families set an extra place at the table for departed family members. It's customary to set up an ancestor's altar at this time with photos and mementos of those who are gone. Divination and spells for spirit contact are popular.

# The Esbats

Just as the year cycles through the sabbats, so do the months embody their esbats. These magical times align to certain colors, herbs, stones, elements, and even signs of the zodiac. As you progress, you'll learn how each moon bears a specific purpose and brings an empowering boost to your magical workings.

## JANUARY (COLD MOON)

Individuality, nonconformity, and communication are all highlighted by this moon. Magic to promote better understanding and clearer communication between individuals will be most beneficial.

## FEBRUARY (QUICKENING MOON)

Cast spells for divination with February's moon. The psychic and spiritual side of life will be highlighted. Balancing dreamy sentimentalism with acceptance of reality will also be something to work on with this moon energy.

## MARCH (STORM MOON)

Spells for reconciliation will be enhanced with March's moon. Work on issues of temperament and aggressiveness. Storm Moon energy can be harnessed for freeing a voice or for binding harmful words.

## APRIL (WIND MOON)

The energy of April's moon is all about manifesting what you've been wishing for. Turn aspirations into reality. Issues of stubbornness are also dealt with, as well as development of courage and some much-needed bravado to do what must be done.

## MAY (FLOWER MOON)

This moon is all about potential, fertility, and growth. Duality is highlighted. Take care to find balance between the light and dark side of everything, including yourself. Cast magic to improve self-esteem and encourage empowerment.

## JUNE (SUN MOON)

The energy for the Sun Moon is about transformations. Cast spells for increase or decrease, to manifest or banish. Take a good look at where change is needed and put your effort there.

## JULY (BLESSING MOON)

Now is the time to implement long-term goals. Highlight magic and desires that will come to fruition during the winter months. Banish procrastination but recognize patience as a blessing.

## AUGUST (CORN MOON)

With August's moon, it's time to cleanse and clear both your physical space and emotional issues. Pave the way for mental solitude and peace in the months that lie ahead.

## SEPTEMBER (HARVEST MOON)

Cast spells to promote love in your life, whether with a new love or reconciling with an old. Work on issues of independence and discernment, always building toward more solid relationships, whether with yourself, family and friends, or your romantic partner.

### OCTOBER (BLOOD MOON)

Cast spells now to promote ambitions, justice, and balance. Work magic to promote your own strengths. Divination and spirit connection are also highlighted with this moon.

### NOVEMBER (MOURNING MOON)

This is the moon for release and emancipation. Recognize what's holding you back and find the courage to disengage or banish the energy. The magic of this moon can be tricky; it embraces the idea of opposites, and irony is its middle name.

### DECEMBER (LONG NIGHTS MOON)

December's moon will reveal the truth and showcase loyalties. Prepare yourself for unexpected revelations: What's in the shadows will be coming into the light.

| | | CORRESPONDENCES | | | |
|---|---|---|---|---|---|
| MONTH | | COLORS | HERBS | STONES | ELEMENTS | ZODIAC |
| | JANUARY | white, indigo, black | patchouli, lavender, pine | garnet, amethyst, red jasper | earth, air | Capricorn, Aquarius |
| | FEBRUARY | light blue, violet | nutmeg, jasmine, myrrh | amethyst, ammolite, purple jade | air, water | Aquarius, Pisces |
| | MARCH | light green, red-violet | calamus, catnip, sage | aquamarine, pink fluorite | water, fire | Pisces, Aries |
| | APRIL | red, gold | allspice, fennel, anise | diamond, kyanite, emerald | fire, earth | Aries, Taurus |
| | MAY | green, pink | apple blossoms, rose, thyme | chrysolite, septarian, malachite | earth, air | Taurus, Gemini |
| | JUNE | orange, yellow-orange | dill, lemongrass, clover | alexandrite, Herkimer diamond | air, water | Gemini, Cancer |
| | JULY | silver, blue-gray | myrrh, sandalwood, lemon balm | ruby, peacock ore | water, fire | Cancer, Leo |

| | CORRESPONDENCES | | | | |
|---|---|---|---|---|---|
| MONTH | COLORS | HERBS | STONES | ELEMENTS | ZODIAC |
| AUGUST | gold, green, yellow | rosemary, calamus, marigold | peridot, green sapphire | earth, air | Leo, Virgo |
| SEPTEMBER | amber, yellow-green, gold | mugwort, marjoram, thyme | sapphire, blood stone | earth, air | Virgo, Libra |
| OCTOBER | orange, dark green | myrrh, basil, cloves | citrine, lilac kunzite | air, water | Libra, Scorpio |
| NOVEMBER | gray, sage green | vanilla, sage, cumin | topaz, smokey quartz | water, fire | Scorpio, Sagittarius |
| DECEMBER | red, white, black | holly, pine, mistletoe | clear quartz, lapis, black tourmaline | fire, water | Sagittarius, Capricorn |

# Do No Harm:
# The Wiccan Viewpoint

"An' it harm none, do what thou will." This is the motto of many Wiccans. However, exactly what this means to each individual practitioner may vary. How the Wiccan Rede is interpreted is subjective. For one practitioner, strong protection magic that may step on a few toes is acceptable, while to another practitioner, it is not.

Every Wiccan knows that the energy one sends out is what comes back, threefold or even tenfold. This still makes the line between what's proper and what's not very hard—if not impossible—to define. As the wise Lirio said in the 1996 film *The Craft*, "True magic is neither black nor white; it's both because nature is both. . . . The only good or bad is in the heart of the witch."

Ask yourself mindfully: What's in your heart? This is going to define your practice of witchcraft. This is going to be the code you live by and the ultimate measure of your integrity, both as an individual and as a practicing Wiccan.

# In Summary

We've covered a lot of magical territory in these pages. You've learned what Wicca, and its practice, is all about and where it came from. You've connected with the energies of the planets, the sun, and the moon and explored how the Wiccan views the year and celebrates the seasons.

Now it's time for you to turn inward. What are your own natural gifts? What are your strengths? How do you relate to Wicca and the practice of witchcraft? It's time for you to become acquainted with your magical self.

## CHAPTER 3

# Discovering Your Wiccan Power

We're going to explore some ways that you can discover your own Wiccan power, something that's accomplished by learning how to center yourself, set solid intentions, and focus your energy effectively before conducting rituals and spell casting. Creating sacred space through circle castings and closings is imperative for the Wiccan practice, as is knowing which tools to use and how to set up your altar. We'll delve into how your power emanates from casting spells, as well as how to manipulate energy to manifest desires, perform rituals, and connect with Spirit. Finally, we'll touch upon creating your personal Book of Shadows—your unique grimoire—where, if you so choose, you'll keep your most empowering spells, learnings, and rituals to build your Wiccan knowledge.

# The Importance of Intention and Self-Centering

It is vital to be grounded and centered before you cast a spell to keep your focus on the energy you need to raise. Your intention must be clearly defined in your mind for you to visualize the outcome—in other words, to make it happen.

## Setting Your Intention

To set your intention properly, you must be able to mentally visualize the positive outcome of a spell *before* it's cast. It's vital to mentally hold on to this image *while* you are casting, and realistic visualization is imperative for you to set an intention.

For example, picture a banana in your mind. Take your time. Once you can clearly see this, move one step closer and peel the banana. Can you still see it clearly? Can you feel it in your hand? Can you feel the texture of the peel as you're pulling it from the banana? Does it make any sound? Can you smell it?

If this is difficult for you to do, keep practicing, and in time you can master it. Use your imagination and several scenarios: Imagine a cat beneath your hand. What does its fur feel like? Can you feel the vibration of its body as it purrs? Imagine a rock in your hand. Is it cold, rough, or smooth? Is it evenly textured or mottled? What does it look like? What color is it, and what shape?

The ability to create a realistic image in your mind and to retain that image while doing other things is imperative to properly set an intention and experience successful spell casting.

## Centering the Self

In order to center yourself for spell casting, you must quiet your mind, intentionally pausing all the internal brain chatter that is normal for most of us. Seat yourself comfortably in a chair, feet flat on the floor, hands loose on your lap, with your palms up. Consciously think about what you're hearing within your mind. What are you thinking about? What are the voices saying? What sounds are you hearing?

The idea is to quiet this sound and turn the voices off. This is something learned gradually because it is incredibly difficult for some people to accomplish. First, try to think of absolutely nothing for just 15 seconds, to keep the mind completely quiet. You'll be surprised—it can be harder than you think! But once you can do this, begin to lengthen this time to 30 seconds, then to one minute and beyond.

Learning to hold this silence is necessary to center yourself, which in turn is necessary to set your intention, stay focused, and commit yourself fully to your practice.

# Casting and Closing Your Wiccan Circle

When you cast a circle, you are creating sacred space. The idea of sacred space is not new, and for the Wiccan, it is no different than the sacred ground of a cemetery yard or the nearest church, synagogue, or mosque for those of other beliefs. It's a space that has been cleared, cleansed, consecrated, and set aside for spiritual activities, including spell and ritual casting and performance. What sets the Wiccan's sacred space apart is the fact that once you are finished with this space, you will close it, dismantling it and releasing the energy contained within.

Keep in mind, though, that you will *not* need to cast a circle for every spell you work or every moment of ritual you may perform, but there are advantages to working within a cast circle. For one, a cast circle will contain the energy you raise until you choose the moment to release it. It will also protect you from unwanted or negative entities that may be drawn to you while you are doing magical things. In short, the sacred circle is your empowered safe zone.

And it's true that a magic circle is a place "outside of time," as one saying goes. You may think you've spent 10 or 15 minutes within your sacred space, only to step out of it and realize that an hour has passed. You may also find the opposite, the feeling that you've been casting and connecting with Spirit for a long period, only to emerge and realize that mere moments have gone by. Some super-sensitive individuals experience physical sensations while inside a cast circle, like feeling flushed and warm or awash in goose bumps. You may also experience similar sensations while in the process of casting or closing a circle.

After your spell has been cast, or your ritual complete, it's important to dismantle the sacred space you've created. Closing a cast circle clears the energy you've raised, sends entities invoked back to their rightful place, and is respectful of the sacredness of this spot of ground you used for however much time you needed it.

Consecrating and blessing your sacred space by opening and closing your magic circle will become second nature with time and dedication. It is as natural to the Wiccan process as lighting a candle or smudging with sage.

You'll find that not all of this book's spells come with the words "cast or close your circle," but your magical instinctive nature will know when this needs to be done, and when you and your work will benefit most from the creation of consecrated space. Follow this instinct always and do what feels right for you.

# Your First Casting Circle

You're going to cast a circle with this ritual to create the sacred space you'll need to work your magic. As mentioned, you don't need to cast a circle for every spell and ritual you perform, but it's integral that you familiarize yourself with casting and closing as a basic step to performing your Wiccan magic. Enjoy this process and experience the empowering energy within this ancient practice.

**Matches (optional)**

**White candle (optional)**

**Incense (optional)**

**Broom**

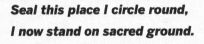

Make sure the space you've selected is physically clean and clear of overall clutter. Light a white candle, along with a favorite type of incense that helps relax and center you, if you like.

With a broom, sweep the floor of the space from east to west while repeating this mantra:

> *Sweep, sweep with this broom,*
> *In this place,*
> *All negativity from this space.*

Stand in the center of the freshly swept area. Beginning at the north, point with your power hand (your dominant hand) and circle clockwise, all the way around the perimeter of your space until you wind up where you started, all the while chanting:

> *Seal this place I circle round,*
> *I now stand on sacred ground.*

# Your First Closing Circle

Once you've worked your magic, cast your spell, or completed your ritual, it's time to respectfully dismantle your sacred space. By doing so, know that the energies you've touched and raised will be sent back where they belong. By including this step in your circle closing, you will be paying respect to the entities and energies that have lent their power and magic to your endeavor. You'll also ensure that there are no loose threads, or undirected and unharnessed energy, to disrupt the flow of manifestation.

Stand in the center of your cast circle.

Raise the arm with your power hand (your dominant hand) above your head. Pointing at the north perimeter of your circle, in one fell swoop, swing your arm counterclockwise above your head to make a complete circle, ending back at the north, all the while chanting:

> *I open now this sacred space,*
> *Releasing all energies to their rightful place.*

# Wiccan Tools to Trust

In the practice of Wicca, you will need a few tools to assist you in the casting of a spell, in the throes of a ceremonial ritual, and in other magical endeavors. These items will be special and sacred to you, often consecrated (or blessed) for their use and definitely cherished.

## Basic Tools

With these simple tools, you'll find a world of magical uses.

### ATHAME (RITUAL KNIFE)

The athame is never used to physically cut anything but rather to direct energy, most often when casting a circle. Keep it separate from knives you use for cutting or other more traditional uses.

### WAND

Similar to the athame, the magic wand directs energy, and some individuals may prefer a wand over an athame. Either works, and many have both of these items in their magical cupboards.

### BROOM

A broom, kept solely for ritual purposes, is used to sweep the ground in preparation for casting a circle. A ritual broom is also used in Wiccan handfastings and weddings, with the couple jumping over the broom at the end of the ceremony. Ritual brooms are often decorated with symbols, ribbons, and other items.

## CHALICE OR CUP

A chalice or cup is used most often for the cakes-and-wine ceremony, and this practice is often incorporated in other Wiccan rituals. Your chalice or cup can be ornate and expensive, made exclusively for Wiccan ceremonies, or it can be a favorite goblet from a local flea market. Whatever you choose should be sacred and special to you.

## CAULDRON

The traditional cauldron is cast iron and is used to hold and burn candles, spell papers, or incense. Much more than a classic symbol of the witch, it's a useful tool that will hold a special place in your magical practice. Although cast iron is traditional for a cauldron, you may improvise with ones made from other metals or alloys as long as the material can withstand heat.

## CRYSTALS AND STONES

A variety of easily sourced and common crystals and stones will be used for their specific, innate energies during spell crafting or rituals. These crystals and stones will decorate your altar, fill a mojo bag, be carried in your pocket or purse, or reside on your tabletops, windowsills, and nightstands. Besides being objects for magical use, they are beautiful and comforting, as well.

## CANDLES

Candles are at the center of many Wiccan spells and rituals. You'll want a variety of candles on hand in a plethora of colors and styles, from tea lights and votives to pillars and tapers. Also, keep candleholders for these various types. You may include male and/or female figure candles for some spells; these can be modified to represent nonbinary or other genders as needed within your specific magic.

### HERBS AND INCENSE

The use of herbs and incense is an integral part of the Wiccan practice. Herbs can be dried, bundled, and hung from the ceiling; dried and crushed to be kept in containers; or found in powdered form in your grocery store's baking aisle in labeled jars. You'll find a variety of incense useful to have on hand in both cone and stick forms.

### OILS

A variety of essential oils, as well as magical oils, will be used to anoint the practitioner, spell papers, candles, stones, jewelry, or other items used in the course of daily rituals or spell crafting. Recipes for magical oils abound and include a base oil, essential oils, herbs, stones, and sometimes other items, like small crystals, as well.

### TAROT CARDS

Tarot cards are a popular form of divination among Wiccans, who often consult the cards as an oracle or before casting a spell to glean insight and wisdom from the universe and Spirit. Tarot cards can be used for personal meditation and journaling. Many practitioners pull a card a day for inspiration and direction. Occasionally, a practitioner may keep a deck of "disposable" tarot cards to be used in spells.

### RUNES

Runes are a form of Norse magic, including Elder Futhark and others, and are another way to connect with daily energy. Some Wiccans pull a rune at the beginning of the day. When used for divination, the runes are all cast together, much in the same way one would toss dice. Only runes that land upright are interpreted, while facedown ones are disregarded.

## CRYSTAL BALL AND SCRYING MIRROR

The crystal ball and scrying mirror are both used to tap into your psychic abilities, see what the future brings, find out hidden information, and give a clear and direct path to the spirit world. Both of these methods employ an inactive approach to psychism, allowing your subconscious mind to work unfettered.

Both divination tools are used in a meditative manner by staring at the surfaces, letting your eyes relax and your inner sight take the lead. The images or insight that is received may be actual images seen within the tools themselves, but they are more likely to be images seen within our own mind's eye, triggered by the alpha, meditative state that this type of divination induces.

## ASTROLOGY

For millennia, people have looked to the stars as a divination tool and as a means of revealing information about individuals and energy around us. You will use astrology to better understand personalities and, in turn, the people, events, and circumstances around you that shape and influence your life. The insightful power of astrology can grant a very clear picture of your personal life, as well as what's to come.

# Your Wiccan Altar

A basic altar setup will include the following important elements.

Three pillar or taper candles for Goddess, Spirit, and God

Cauldron

Chalice or cup

Wand

Lighter or matches

Incense

Pentagram, either ceramic plaque or pendant

Small bowl of water

Small bowl of salt

Book of Shadows

Athame

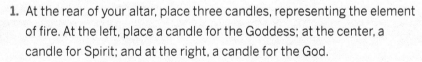

1. At the rear of your altar, place three candles, representing the element of fire. At the left, place a candle for the Goddess; at the center, a candle for Spirit; and at the right, a candle for the God.

2. At the center of your altar, place the cauldron.

3. To the left of the cauldron, place a chalice or cup.

4. To the right of the cauldron, place your wand, a lighter or matches, and incense. The incense will represent the element of air.

5. In front of the cauldron, place a pentagram, which can be in the form of a small ceramic plaque or a simpler piece of jewelry like a pendant. To the left of the pentagram, place a small dish of water, which will represent the element of water. To the right of the pentagram, place a small bowl of salt, which will represent the element of earth.

6. Ahead of the pentagram and bowls, directly in front of you, leave a space clear for a work area.

7. To the left of this cleared space, place your Book of Shadows.

8. To the right of this work area, place your athame.

# Spells, Rituals, and Keeping a Book of Shadows or Grimoire

Within this section, we will take a look at spells, which are magical workings to manifest something that you desire, and rituals, which are ceremonies to connect with Spirit, acknowledge an esbat or sabbat, or celebrate a holiday. Finally, we will explore the Book of Shadows, an invaluable reference that is often a handwritten book filled with personalized spells and notes, and sometimes the witch's deepest thoughts and dreams. Finally, we'll look at how you can start your own Book of Shadows as you learn and grow in your magical practice.

## Spells

Casting a spell means that you are using the energy of your mind and will, along with material items such as candles, incense, magical oils, and crystals, to move energy in a way that physically manifests your desired outcome in the real world. There are some practitioners, called adepts, who can raise and move spellcasting energy without using any tools other than their mind. I have yet to meet one in my own practice, but you may well meet (or be) one such person. The tools of witchcraft are triggers for those of us who need some help raising and directing magical energy.

Within the world, you can easily find a plethora of written spells, both in books and online formats, written by experienced practitioners who have graciously offered their work for use by others. It is perfectly acceptable to use their spells; however, much like a kitchen recipe, it's equally acceptable to tweak another's spell to make it your own. As you move deeper into your practice, you'll likely find the best spells for you are the spells you write yourself, in your own intention and unique expression.

## Rituals

A ritual, or ceremony, is very focused, with a specific intention or objective for celebration or acknowledgment. When you are in the midst of a ritual, you are touching base with the spiritual aspect of Wicca. You are not working to manifest something for yourself or those around you, but instead you are honoring Spirit, the magical energies of the universe, or one of life's significant milestones.

When you participate in a ritual, you are strengthening the connection you have to your spiritual practice, to the deities that you acknowledge, and to all the natural energies and entities that come together in the magical world to make it work.

## Book of Shadows or Grimoire

A Book of Shadows, or grimoire, can be as simple (like a notebook, journal, or binder) or ornate (leatherbound, decorated, or with an embossed, handstitched cover) as you prefer. The book contains spells that you have found and recorded for future use or spells you've written and crafted specifically for your own use. Many Wiccans also include notes, personal journaling entries, a record of spells cast and outcomes, divination information, specific information on herbs and stones, magical recipes, mementos of their practice, lists of magical to-dos, and so on.

Your Book of Shadows contains the fingerprint of your own unique magical practice. It can become a precious, very personal item to be passed down through a family, or through a coven.

That said, does a Book of Shadows have to be an expensive leather-bound ornate piece of art? Not in the least! My Book of Shadows is a three-ring binder that has grown to tremendous proportions over the years but remains as accessible as ever thanks to its simple format. It's easy to add or remove pages or move whole sections around, as well as inexpensive and very versatile.

To start your own Book of Shadows, pick up supplies as simple as a three-ring binder, notebook paper, and dividers. Should you prefer something more ornate, such as a keepsake journal, that's entirely your call, and these can be found in any number of small magical shops or online marketplaces. Off you go!

# In Summary

In this chapter, you've learned how to cast and open a circle, the differences between spells and rituals, and the benefits of keeping your own Book of Shadows. You've become familiar with the tools of the trade and how to use them, as well as how to arrange a simple altar space. You've successfully reached one of many milestones on your journey through Wicca.

Now that you're aware of your own magical power and potential, it's time to reach for the moon and advance to the next level to explore the many ways you can harness this power for your benefit, and for others, as well.

## CHAPTER 4

# The Ways to Practice Wicca

Earlier, we discussed the fact that Wicca is unique to each practitioner. In this chapter, we're going to explore the Wiccan way up close and personal. You're going to progress even further on this journey by learning how to write your own spells and craft your own magic. We'll also discuss where to practice your craft and what to wear when you do.

It's time to get inspired as you gain the knowledge to develop and grow spiritually on your magical journey.

# The Wiccan Coven

A coven is a group of Wiccans who meet on a regular basis to work together, celebrate the sabbats and esbats, cast spells, share in other magical workings, and mark life's milestones with rituals. They may or may not adhere to a particular tradition or incorporate a degree system within their group. There may or may not be a recognized hierarchy within a coven, which would include a high priest and priestess. They may meet in person physically, or they may be an online coven that convenes over the Internet.

The number of coven members varies according to the group and its rules and preferences; the ideal number of members for a coven is 3, 6, 9, or 13. There must be more than 2 members to officially be a coven, but it's not desirable to allow a group to grow to a point where it is unmanageable. There is magical significance in the number three and the multiples of that number, most notably mentioned in the phrase at the end of spell casting, "By the awful awesome power of three times three." Contrary to the mundane world, in Wicca the number 13 is considered lucky and the maximum number of members for a coven.

A coven can provide a wonderful support system for the newbie by having more experienced members available to answer questions, provide resources, and help with hands-on learning. A coven may also ensure a higher collective energy level and grant the ability to raise energy faster. Within a coven, you've got a whole group of people all on the same page, all focused on the same intention. Look out, universe.

But a coven may not be right for all beginner Wiccans. Some of the disadvantages may include the difficulty of trying to schedule dates for all this magical activity so that it works for every member. Like anything else, a coven may also run into personality conflicts and ego issues. Wiccans are only human, after all, and there's always a chance that not everyone in a group will contribute to a happy dynamic.

If you're a solitary and interested in finding a coven, a good place to start is with occult websites and social websites. You'll usually find a listing of covens at these pages, including physical locations for real-world covens and links to online covens, along with their requirements for members and their personal philosophies and practices. You might also think about starting your own coven, either with a group of like-minded friends in the real world or with the launching of a website or social media source to help others as you learn together.

## The Solitary Wiccan

The solitary Wiccan is one who chooses to work solo. There are a vast number of newcomer practitioners who prefer this route and have found this option refreshing after coming off of other spiritual avenues that include considerable amounts of person-to-person contact and long-established rules. This is just one shade of the beauty of Wicca and the amazing world of witchcraft; you have personal choices and options.

The benefits of solo practice are many. For one, you have an opportunity to really learn about yourself, a process that can be simpler when we have some distance from other people, aren't confined by anyone's expectations, and don't bear the brunt of another's criticisms.

As a solitary Wiccan, you can also develop a regular practice that is in tune with your own preferences, timetable, and modes of magic. You choose what's important for you to acknowledge, celebrate, or manifest. Though many Wiccans openly and freely practice their craft and acknowledge it with others, there are some who, for a variety of reasons, prefer to keep their Wiccan practice a private matter. As a solitary, it's easier to stay in the broom closet, so to speak.

As with a coven and its group work, solitary work may not be for every new Wiccan. Some challenges include finding ways to stay motivated and determined to see things through—to finish what you start—and finding self-directed resources for learning and study. However, if you're already an introverted person who likes to do things their own way, the solitary path may be just the thing for you. Not everyone is a team player and, in the Wiccan world, that's okay.

# Spell Writing in Your Own Words

The power and ability to manifest spells comes down to our intentions, our emotions, and the words we choose to pair them with. What could be more powerful, more apt to make your spell crafting successful, than to use your own words? We should never be afraid of expressing ourselves. Who is going to have more energy, more determination, or more emotion involved in something you desire than yourself?

Writing a spell is similar in some ways to writing a recipe.

First, think of the correspondences that go with your intention: the colors, magical timing, herbs and stones, deity, moon phase, or element. Any or all of these connections (and more) can be included in a spell, and the more magical correspondences that come together, the better.

Second, think about *exactly* what it is you want to manifest. If you're going to incorporate this as part of your spell paper, make sure you've thought it through and can see it clearly. Be precise, not vague. It's often been said that, although the energy raised during a spell may be effective, it is not intelligent. It's just pure energy—it follows the path of least resistance.

Third, start writing. Write down your intention automatically, without censoring yourself or worrying about construction and punctuation, and read it back to yourself out loud. Think about how it sounds. Is it compact, consistent, and to the point? Is it precise?

Finally, take your time to rewrite and revise the spell if need be, to make it flow with rhyming words and powerful rhythm or to create a solid and direct soliloquy. This is your opportunity to pour your emotions and energy directly into the mechanism that powers your ability to manifest your intention, *your* spell.

Always remember that there is power in your words.

# The Wiccan's Settings

The choice of where you celebrate rituals, craft spells, and otherwise connect with Spirit is a decision left up to each practitioner, taking into consideration preferences and availability. Once a physical place has been prepared, time and space are transcended within a cast circle. Magic can be made anywhere, but let's look into ways to transcend no matter where you are.

## Outdoors

The witch's deep and mystical connection to nature is elemental with a potent outdoor connection when it comes to rituals and spell crafting. What better way is there to get grounded and use natural energies than to set up a sacred space or an altar in the great outdoors, beneath a tree, near a stream, or in a garden?

The biggest disadvantage to setting up your sacred space outdoors is the lack of privacy, especially if you have neighbors nearby. The sight of a robed individual brandishing an athame in the backyard might raise some eyebrows, so only work your magic outdoors when you are most comfortable, safe, and at ease.

## Indoors

Some witches maintain an entire room in their home for Wiccan purposes, complete with a permanent circle painted on the floor, a table for altar purposes, and shelves and cupboards for magical supplies. Other practitioners will content themselves with a single bookshelf or windowsill; and for some it may be a complete altar kept on a small tray that can be easily concealed beneath a bed or sofa.

The most obvious advantage of practicing witchcraft indoors is privacy. You are free to work unencumbered from prying eyes and curious neighbors. You may dance around your cast circle in nothing but a smile.

## Ritual Space

Whichever venue you choose for your magical practice, it takes some effort to set up and prepare the area. If you're working outdoors, you might think about a small suitcase or backpack to haul your things to the spot you've chosen. If you're working indoors, of course, you won't have as far to carry everything, which makes things a bit easier. Setting up sacred space anywhere takes physical energy, and this energy will work with you as you build toward a ritual or the manifestation of a spell.

When you've finished your ritual, after you've cast your spell, be prepared to clear this space as a courtesy to those who come after you and to show respect for the space. Leave no trace of your presence. Clear the physical objects and remnants of your magical endeavor, as well as the spiritual aspects. Close your circle and be on your way.

# The Wiccan's Wear

There are several ways that you can dress for rituals, ceremonies, or other magical endeavors. From clothing to empowered jewelry and adornments, we'll look at some of these choices here.

## What to Wear (or Not Wear)

Just as practitioners of other spiritualities get dressed up for services and rituals, so does the Wiccan, whether solitary or part of a coven, with special clothes and accessories to enhance their experience.

## CEREMONIAL DRESS

You can find beautiful ceremonial robes online and in new-age Wiccan shops, and you'll likely see inexpensive and simple, as well as more elaborate and pricey, robes. Some practitioners who are handy with needle and thread make their own robes. Ceremonial robes are worn for formal rituals or ceremonies like handfastings, wiccanings, sabbat rituals, and full-moon celebrations.

## EMPOWERED ADORNMENTS

Every witch will have magical jewelry that is consecrated for specific purposes and intentions, be it a ring, a pair of earrings, or a pendant. These are often worn every day as protection, as an outward symbol of personal beliefs, or in honor of Spirit or a particular deity.

Essential oils can also be incorporated as part of your adornment for rituals and spell casting. For example, sage is cleansing, patchouli is earthy and sensuous, rose is used for love spells, and calendula enhances communication. Do you have a particular essential oil that helps you connect with a specific intention, magical practice, or deity? If so, wear this scent as part of your ritual adornment.

## WORKING SKYCLAD

There are some practitioners that prefer to work skyclad, more commonly known as naked. Working skyclad is a very personal decision, and something done only in a safe, secure, and very private area. Being naked for rituals or spell casting is *not* required in the practice of witchcraft, and it is *not* something any practitioner should be pressured into by a group. If you become involved with a coven, this is an important point to be very clear about. If working skyclad is part of their tradition and practice, and you don't feel comfortable with it, find another coven. Be true to your sense of safety and self, and your own practice, above all!

# Key Wiccan Symbols and Language

Within the Wiccan tradition, there are words and many symbols that carry power and energy. Some of these are easily recognizable, and others are more enigmatic. Among practitioners, whether solitary or coven-related, a magical name will become your mantle. Within the world of witchcraft, everything carries magical energy.

## Wiccan Symbols

You'll find some of the most commonly used and recognizable Wiccan symbols and terms here.

### CELTIC KNOT

Sometimes known as the triquetra, the Celtic knot is made from a single, uninterrupted line and represents sets of three. This symbol may also represent the triple goddess. Interestingly, the Celtic knot is on the cover of the Book of Shadows in the television series *Charmed*.

### CELTIC SHIELD KNOT

A set of four Celtic knot designs incorporated into one and closely resembling a medieval knight's shield, this is a symbol used for protection and warding. In Celtic traditions of witchcraft, the basic square shape may represent the four elements.

### CRESCENT MOON

The waning crescent represents the Goddess at the Crone stage; the waxing crescent represents the Goddess as the Maiden. The waning crescent is the moon coming out of the full phase and beginning its journey to the dark moon. The waxing crescent is the moon coming out of the dark phase and beginning its growth to a full moon.

### FULL MOON

The full moon represents the Goddess as the Mother. It's this energy that is ripe and fertile, encompassing the power of manifestation. The full moon represents an especially sacred time for those who identify with the feminine, highlighting completion and fulfillment.

### HEKATE'S WHEEL

This is a popular symbol among Wiccan feminists, particularly Dianic Wiccans, and represents the three faces of the Goddess. The labyrinth, the spiraling maze, references the serpent and the power of life.

### HORNED GOD

Most often a male figure with the horns of a stag, this symbol recognizes the masculine energy of the pagan god and is often associated with the Celtic god Cernunnos.

### PENTACLE

The pentacle is a five-point star, representing earth, air, fire, water, and Spirit.

### PENTAGRAM

The pentagram is the pentacle enclosed in a circle. Encircling the pentacle, thereby creating the pentagram, crafts a powerful talisman. The pentagram is often worn as a pendant or ring, used upon the pagan altar to represent the element of Earth, or placed within a space for protection.

## SEPTOGRAM

This seven-point star is a symbol used to invoke protection and harmony. Also known as the "fairy star," it represents the seven chakras, seven elements, and seven days of the week.

## SOLAR CROSS

The four-armed cross within a circle represents the sun, as well as the earth's journey through the four seasons.

## TRIANGLE

There are four versions of the triangle that represent the four elements. The upright triangle represents fire, the inverted triangle stands for water, an upright triangle with a line drawn through it represents air, and an inverted triangle with a line drawn through it symbolizes earth.

## TRIPLE MOON

This symbol represents the three stages of the moon and the three faces of the Goddess: Maiden, Mother, and Crone. This image is depicted with the full moon in the center and the crescents on either side, with their points outward.

## TRIPLE SPIRAL

The triple spiral, also called a triskele, represents earth, sea, and sky. It's formed with three small spirals in a circular shape.

## WEDJAT

This symbol, also known as the Eye of Horus, is an Egyptian glyph representing protection and healing. The offspring of the sun god, Ra, and the Egyptian goddess, Isis, Horus became a physician, according to legend, hence the connection of this symbol to healing.

### WHEEL OF THE YEAR
The eight-spoked Wheel of the Year represents our journey through the calendar year, with the change of seasons and the celebration of pagan holidays.

## Wiccan Terms

You'll find these terms when casting some spells or conducting some rituals, so read on for concise illuminations on just what they mean.

### DEOSIL
*Deosil* means clockwise, and in Wicca the term describes the act of moving in a clockwise motion. Usually, the reference is associated with casting a circle, but it can refer to stirring ingredients to further empower a spell or ritual, as well.

### WIDDERSHINS
*Widdershins* means counterclockwise, and Wiccans use it to indicate moving in a counterclockwise motion. This term is usually used in reference to circle casting but can also refer to stirring ingredients.

## Your Wiccan Name

When you reach the point of your first-level initiation in a coven or your first solo year of study and the time for self-initiation, you'll want to choose a magical name as part of the process. When you are deciding upon your magical name, consider totem animals, herbs, stones, trees, and pagan deities, as well as other natural things in the world for inspiration.

Note that some people do not reveal their magical name but choose to use it only during private rituals, ceremonies, or spell casting. It's said that Spirit and the energies the witch summons during ritual or spell casting will recognize them when they call upon them using the magical name they took at their initiation. It becomes a private connection between the witch and the powers that be.

# Reading the Wiccan Rainbow

Color is a powerful source of energy, and every color has its own unique tone that relates to very specific intentions. You can incorporate the use of color in your Wiccan practice through candles, stones, altar cloths, ritual clothing, and jewelry.

**Red** is used to represent the element of fire and is connected to Tuesday and the planet Mars. It's used for love and passion, lust, and expediting the rapid movement of energy, speeding things along.

**Orange** is connected to Sunday and the sun. It's God energy, used for healing, success, and fertility magic. It's also a very powerful warrior energy, indispensable when courage, strength, and stamina are needed.

**Yellow** is used to represent the element of air and is connected to Wednesday and the planet Mercury. Its energy is used for communication, as well as to inspire creativity and enhance mental endeavors.

**Green** is used to represent the element of earth and is connected to Friday and the planet Venus. Its energy lends itself to health, healing, beauty, prosperity, and things of a material nature.

**Blue** is used to represent the element of water and is connected to Monday and the celestial body of the moon. It's Goddess energy, used to enhance psychic powers and dream recall, as well as to strengthen the powers of divination.

**Purple** is connected to Thursday and the planet Jupiter. This energy is used for spells dealing with financial and legal issues, as well as expansion and growth.

# In Summary

Congratulations on reaching this point in your magical journey! You're now ready to roll up your sleeves and start casting some spells. We're going to be looking at spells for a wide range of purposes, including harmony, healing, and attraction, as well as spells that energize, encourage, and welcome abundance. We'll explore spells that will benefit friends and family, as well as spells of protection, should this be the energy you need.

Put your witch hat on, for there's work to be done and magic to be made.

# PART TWO

# Spells

In this section, you'll find almost any spell a newbie Wiccan might need, whether for attraction, affection, attention, or protection. If you're in need of some magical help for friends and family, you'll find spells of health, healing, and, best of all, harmony. Get ready to flex your magical muscles as you progress through these spells, casting magic that will inspire you and transform the lives of yourself and your loved ones.

## CHAPTER 5

# Spells for Attraction and Affection

One of the most popular reasons for casting spells is to bring something you desire, whether a specific manifestation of something or a greater magically empowered change. You'll find plenty of desires in life for this kind of magic, and it's not just love and romance, though that's a popular reason. The following spells will be cast to attract something to you and to encourage love and affection from those around you, whether romantic, platonic, or otherwise.

# Setting Your Intention

These spells are about attracting those things you want for yourself. Think about what it is you really want, then think some more, because the old saying "Be careful what you wish for" definitely comes to mind. If there's something you truly desire, know that as a Wiccan, you have the magical power to attain it.

In order to successfully manifest your desires, you need to see, hear, taste, and smell them as though they already exist by using the visualizing power of your mind.

What is it you want? A lover? Can you feel their lips on yours? Can you smell their sweet warm breath on your face? Money? Do you feel the weight of coins in your hand? Can you hear them jingle? Whatever you seek to manifest, first set it within your mind and make it as real as you can. With that, embark upon your spell or ritual work with confidence and conviction.

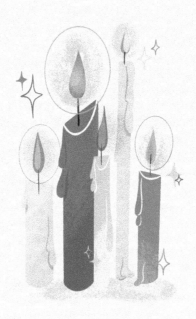

# To Find a New Love

This spell is intended to bring a romantic partner into your life, but it is not a spell targeting a specific individual. Your energy will work with Spirit to draw to you the person who will most resonate with you for a successful long-term romantic partnership. Open your energy and your heart to unexpected possibilities. Use rose oil for love, gardenia oil for love and commitment, jasmine oil to open the heart chakra, and rose quartz for love and the heart chakra.

**Red votive candle**

**Essential oil: rose, gardenia, or jasmine**

**Fireproof plate**

**Long-stemmed red rose**

**2 rose quartz stones**

**Matches**

**Incense: rose, gardenia, or jasmine**

**Paper and pen**

**Fireproof container or cauldron**

**Red velvet bag**

1. Anoint a red candle with essential oil and place it on a fireproof plate. Remove the petals from a single red rose and place them in a circle around the outer edges of the plate. Place two rose quartz stones next to the base of your candle.

2. Light the candle and incense.

3. On a sheet of paper, list the qualities that you are looking for in a romantic partner, such as a good sense of humor, honesty, integrity, gentleness, an ability to compromise, shared interests, and the physical attributes that you find appealing.

4. Hold this paper over the flame until it ignites, then drop it into your cauldron or fireproof container to burn to ash.

5. When the spell is complete, gather all the ash from the spell paper, the stones, the candle wax, and the rose petals, and place these remains in a red velvet bag. Keep this bag hidden beneath your bed until that special person enters your life.

# To Find a Lost Object

It's frustrating to lose anything, but it's especially upsetting when we've lost an item that is valuable or necessary and have no idea where to start looking. If this is your situation, this is the spell you need to focus your energy on what you need to find, no matter what it is you've lost. Pendulums can be found online or at your local new-age shop. With a wide variety available, they can be made of metal, crystals, stones, and even botanical elements, like dried nuts.

**Paper and pen**          **Table and chair**

**White votive candle**    **Pendulum**

**Matches**

1. On a square sheet of paper, draw a large circle. Divide this circle into sections, as you would a pie. The number of sections you have will depend upon the number of locations that you can think of to search. Within each blank section, write down a location, such as bathroom, bedroom, garage, vehicle, office desk, and so on.

2. When you're ready, light a white votive candle and seat yourself comfortably at a table. Determine which direction the pendulum will move to indicate an affirmative answer.

3. Hold the pendulum over each location, one at a time, and say, "Is this where my _____ is?" Keep moving from section to section until the pendulum gives you a yes.

4. An alternative method is to hold the pendulum in the center of your circle, ask where the missing item is, and wait to see which direction the pendulum will swing, revealing where you can find the missing object.

5. For some people this may take more than one session. If it does, extinguish your candle until you're ready to give it another go. Success depends upon how much practice you've had with your pendulum and what frame of mind you're in.

# To Attract a Positive Coworker or Business Partner

The work world is made much easier when others resonate with our energy, whether it's a coworker we rub shoulders with every day or we're in need of a reliable business partner. For this spell, you'll create a mojo bag, a pretty little bag in which you'll place items for your spell work. You'll use herbs (like patchouli for prosperity, money, and an earth element; cinnamon to attract money; mint for money and prosperity; and marjoram for prosperity and success) and stones (aventurine for health, wealth, and the earth element and tigereye for luck and business/legal success) to help attract the right person.

**Green pillar candle**

**Essential oil: patchouli or cinnamon**

**Fireproof plate**

**Matches**

**Incense: patchouli or cinnamon**

**Scissors**

**Paper and pen**

**Stones: aventurine, tigereye**

**Herbs: dried patchouli, mint, marjoram**

**Green velvet or cotton bag**

1. Anoint a green candle with essential oil and place it on a fireproof plate. Light the candle and the incense.

2. Cut a sheet of paper into small strips. On each strip, write the qualities that you're looking for in a coworker or business partner.

3. Put the paper, stones, and herbs into a green bag. Add three drops of essential oil.

4. Extinguish the candle and incense when you've finished creating your mojo bag.

5. Keep this bag tucked away at your workplace, in your vehicle, or in your purse or backpack.

# To Regain Lost Affection

Whether you've fallen out of grace with a romantic partner, family member, or friend, this spell will help warm the heart of someone who no longer has warm regard for you. Even a simple misunderstanding can warp a connection, and this spell will help set that energy right. This spell, which includes rose petals to invite love or pink geraniums for affection and friendship, works best with reciprocal energy, meaning that the individual in question also desires a reconnection. It is not advised to use this spell to manipulate an individual against their will.

**Straight pin, small knife, or pen**

**Pink pillar candle**

**White pillar candle**

**Fireproof plate or platter**

**Herbs: crushed pink rose petals or pink geranium blossoms**

**Matches**

**Red ribbon, 6 to 8 inches long**

1. Using a straight pin, knife blade, or pen, inscribe a pink candle with your name. Inscribe a white candle with the name of the person whose affection you're trying to regain.

2. Set the candles on opposite sides of a fireproof platter or plate.

3. Sprinkle a line of crushed petals or blossoms between the two candles.

4. For seven consecutive nights, light both candles, burning them for at least 10 minutes, then extinguish them until the next night. Every night, before lighting the candles, move them a bit closer to each other. Imagine them walking through the trail of crushed flower petals to meet each other.

5. On the seventh night, make sure the candles have met in the center of the plate and are closely touching before lighting them.

6. When you extinguish the candles on the seventh night, without moving them, tie them together with a red ribbon.

7. Set this plate beneath your bed and leave it there until you hear from the person whose name you inscribed on the white candle. After that, discard the candles by throwing them in the trash or finding a suitable spot to bury them, such as a garden or your own yard.

# To Attract a Job

When it comes to our working lives, many people desire a dream job that connects with them, or a job that encompasses something they are interested in or love. But there are times you may find yourself at a juncture in life or in a precarious financial situation where any job will do for the moment. This is a spell for such moments.

**Green pillar candle**

**Matches**

**Scissors**

**$1 bill or play money**

**Mason jar with lid**

**Personal effects such as your fingernail clippings, a snippet of hair, or**

**a paper with your name on it**

**Job-related items connected to the specific job you want or a general job that interests you, such as soil from the place of business, price tags from items purchased there, or napkins or flyers from the business**

1. Light a green candle.

2. If using a $1 bill, roll it and place it into the mason jar. If using play money, cut the play money into tiny strips and place them into the mason jar.

3. Next, add your own personal effects to the jar. As always, remember that the more personal the item is, the stronger the energy of the spell will be.

4. Add something that will help you attract the type of job that you're looking for. If you have more than one idea in mind, add as many items as you need.

5. Seal this jar with dripping wax from the green candle.

6. You can keep this jar in your vehicle so that it experiences daily movement, or set it next to your front door and shake it once a day. Shaking the contents will keep it activated and working.

# To Attract Good Luck to Your Home

Some people just seem to be naturally blessed with good luck throughout their lives, while for others it's elusive. These simple spell suggestions include white sage for cleansing, bamboo for good luck and prosperity, and acorns for good luck. Raise the vibrations to bring good luck back into your home and your life with any, or all, of these spells.

**White sage**

**Matches**

**Bamboo**

**Small mason jar with lid**

**Acorns**

**Hammer and nail**

**Horseshoe**

1. **White sage:** Burn sage regularly. When you burn sage in a space, it clears out negative energy, which can bring bad luck. Bundles of sage can be purchased online. You can also usually find them at your nearest new-age or candle and incense shop, or you can grow and dry your own.

2. **Bamboo:** Bring a vase of live bamboo into your home. Bamboo brings not only good luck with its presence, but also financial prosperity, which can only add to the positive energy and good fortune. You can find pots of live bamboo at most garden centers.

3. **Acorns:** To bring positive energy into your home, fill a mason jar with acorns. The Druids believed that acorns brought good luck, and they would carry an acorn with them for this purpose. You may find acorns at your local new-age shop in the herb section, or look for an oak tree near you and start collecting acorns on your daily walk.

4. **Horseshoe:** Using a hammer and nail, hang a horseshoe above your front door to bless all who enter or exit with good luck. It's most commonly believed that the horseshoe should be hung with the open end facing upward. It's said that hanging a horseshoe upside down allows all the luck to pour out and the horseshoe loses its potency. You can buy horseshoes online or at your nearest farm-and-garden supply store.

# To Bring Prophetic Dreams

Everyone dreams, though not all people remember theirs or are able to distinguish between aimless dreams and those that bring messages from the other side. This spell will help you attract prophetic dreams to your subconscious and aid dream recall after you wake. You'll make a mojo bag to keep inside your pillowcase with several herbs, including chamomile for peaceful sleep, lavender to encourage relaxation and ease anxiety, and mugwort for heightened intuition and spirit contact. Your mojo bag will also hold blue lace agate for serenity, apatite to help connect with emotions, or lapis to heighten intuition. For the most beneficial effect, record your dreams in a dream journal for further reflection and learning.

**Blue velvet or cotton bag**

**Stone: blue lace agate, apatite, or lapis**

**Herbs: chamomile, lavender, mugwort**

**Personal effects belonging to a deceased loved one, such as a piece of jewelry, a button from their clothing, a scarf, a wallet, or similar things (optional)**

**Essential oil: lavender**

1. In a blue velvet or cotton bag, place a blue stone and the chamomile, lavender, and mugwort.

2. If you're seeking to attract prophetic messages from a particular spirit, add something that connects with that loved one's energy, such as a button from their clothing, a ring or earring, a piece of paper with their handwriting on it, a snippet of hair, or another small item.

3. Anoint the bag with lavender essential oil.

4. Place this bag in your pillowcase. About once a month, on or near the night of a full moon, anoint the bag with lavender essential oil.

5. Sweet dreams.

# To Attract a Familiar

For some, our familiar is a pet, a loving and cherished companion. For others, their connection to an animal familiar is purely magical, bringing them closer to such wild animals as dolphins, whales, bison, wolves, and bears. This is a spell to attract both to you, either in the form of a loving fur baby or a unique, mystical wild form. Before you begin, ask yourself what animal it is that you feel an affinity for. Dogs? Cats? Birds? Reptiles? Something else? Once you know, proceed with your spell, which calls upon a white candle, as well as sandalwood for purification and manifestation and lavender to enhance serenity and intuition.

**Pictures or illustrations of animals (from magazines or printed from online sources)**

**Glue**

**Large white poster board**

**Pen or pencil**

**Small nail or tack**

**White tea candle**

**Incense: sandalwood or lavender**

1. To begin, create a manifestation board.

2. Using animal images and glue, assemble a collage of familiars on poster board. Be sure to leave space around each image and write your thoughts or wishes around each creature. Once you've finished, let the collage dry. Tack or nail this board on a wall somewhere in your home where you see it every day.

3. On the seventh day after you've created this board, light a white candle and incense and burn it before you go to bed. Use this time for quiet meditation and visualization to connect with the spirit of your familiar.

4. Within a moon phase, the animal that is your familiar will be revealed to you.

## CHAPTER 6

# Spells for Harmony and Healing

Being healthy in body, mind, and spirit is our first goal, since everything else in life is secondary if we're unwell in any of these areas. You'll find spells here that address all three of these aspects that may need healing, as well as spells to keep our lives harmonious and happy.

It's vital to remember, however, that spells of health and healing are not intended to take the place of a medical doctor, specialist, or professional therapist but should be used to complement appropriate medical and therapeutic treatment.

# Setting Your Intention

Setting intentions for a spell that encompasses healing and recovery can be as simple as focusing on that part of us that needs healing, whether it's a physical condition, an emotional trauma, or a spiritual wound. Maintaining harmony in life may mean that there are individuals or situations in our lives we must banish. There may be boundaries that we have to put up and maintain for harmony to prevail, and these situations must be faced realistically for us to set our intentions.

A few ways to set your intentions might include the following:

- Recording your intention in a journal for this purpose

- Creating a mantra or chant and speaking it every evening over the course of several days

- Using a form of divination, such as tarot cards, to gain perspective on your intention and desired outcome

As you set your intention, utilize one or more of these methods to specifically define your personal situation and to highlight the remedy needed to bring healing to fruition. As with your other intention setting, use keen visualization before beginning your spell or ritual work as well, keeping it centered in your mind.

# Setting Boundaries for Negative People in School or the Workplace

No matter how hard you try to maintain a positive life, sometimes you will run into individuals who do nothing but cause trouble and discord. You may also find yourself in a situation where you are touched by such people and their negative energy on a daily basis. With this spell, you'll set up some personal energetic boundaries to help temper the negative fallout.

The mojo bag you'll create will contain all the energy to help manifest your intention. Within your bag, blue kunzite supports emotional stability, chalcedony brings peace and harmony, and sodalite enhances connection with emotions and the element of water. You'll also include lavender for calm emotions and to ease anxiety, chamomile to aid relaxation, and skullcap for protection.

**Stones: blue kunzite, chalcedony, sodalite**

**Small blue cotton or gauze bag**

**Herbs: lavender, chamomile, skullcap**

**1 teaspoon sea salt**

**Paper and pen**

**Dove's feather, or a white feather of your choice**

**Essential oil: lavender**

1. Place the stones in a blue bag to inspire peace and harmony.

2. Add the herbs and sea salt.

3. Create a small spell paper for your intention. Write: *Your negative energy can't touch me, keep your distance, so mote it be!*

4. Place this in the bag. Add the feather to the bag.

5. Anoint the bag with lavender essential oil. Keep this in a desk or locker at your school or workplace. If this isn't possible, take it with you daily on your person or in your vehicle.

# Healing from Abuse

Abuse can leave scars that will forever affect a survivor, potentially influencing their relationships and how they interact with others. This spell is meant to banish feelings of guilt, reclaim personal power, and help the survivor understand that future healthy relationships and connections are possible. It draws on dragon's blood to support protection and enhance boundaries, eucalyptus to bring clarity and healing, and sandalwood for cleansing. It is not a substitute for therapy, treatment, and counseling, but it can help encourage and aid the healing process.

**Red votive candle**

**Essential oil: dragon's blood or eucalyptus**

**Fireproof plate**

**Matches**

**Incense: dragon's blood or sandalwood**

**Table and chair**

**2 sheets of paper and a pen**

**Cauldron or fireproof receptacle**

1. On a Tuesday, on or just after a waning gibbous moon, anoint a red candle with essential oil. Place the candle on a fireproof plate. Light the candle and the incense.

2. Seat yourself at a table with pen and paper. On one sheet of paper, write down the emotions that are causing you the most difficulty now. Write down what it is in your daily life that triggers bad memories or anxiety. On the other piece of paper, write the following affirmations: *I am powerful. I am in control of my life. I have come full circle. My journey leads me back to a complete and happy life.* Write down future wishes for yourself.

3. Hold each piece of paper to the flame and allow it to ignite. Drop both papers into your cauldron or fireproof receptacle and let them burn to ash.

4. Extinguish the candle.

5. Collect the cooled ashes and hold them in the palm of your hand. Step outside and blow the ash off your hand into the air. As you do this, visualize that you are releasing negative energy and sending into the universe a blueprint for how you want your daily life to be, free from abuse or mistreatment and fully empowered.

# Healing from Mental Trauma

This spell is meant to establish mental calm, release anxiety, and bring refreshed, peaceful energy after trauma. A witch's bottle dates back to 17th-century England and is a uniquely wonderful way to cast a spell by filling a glass jar with magical ingredients. This special bottle can be kept as long as you like and will contain sandalwood for peace, rosemary to bring cleansing energy, mint to support healing, and sage to purify. Crystals complement the herbs, including aventurine to promote healing, turquoise for mental clarity, and clear quartz crystal to connect with all seven chakras. If you so choose, include personal effects, as well. Magical spells are meant to be used in conjunction with, not instead of, medical and therapeutic treatments, so let this complement your overall healing practices.

**Blue votive or taper candle**

**Incense: sandalwood or another scent of your choice**

**Matches**

**Pint mason jar and lid**

**¼ cup sea salt**

**¼ cup charcoal**

**Herbs: 3 tablespoons dried rosemary, 3 tablespoons crushed mint, 3 tablespoons**

**powdered sage**

**Stones: aventurine, turquoise, clear quartz crystal**

**Personal effects such as a small snipping of your hair, fingernail clippings, or a name paper (optional)**

**Religious medal or pendant, whatever resonates with you spiritually (optional)**

1. Light the candle and incense.
2. In the pint mason jar, place a layer of sea salt, followed by a layer of charcoal, each layer about one inch thick.
3. Sprinkle in the herbs: first a layer of rosemary, then mint, then sage.
4. Lay three stones on top of the layers: aventurine, turquoise, and clear quartz crystal.

5. If you choose, add your personal effects and a religious medal or pendant that resonates with you.

6. Cap the jar and seal it with the dripping blue wax from your candle. The bottle is empowered with healing energy and should be kept in a safe place close to you as you work through the healing process.

# Magical Oil for Overall Healing

Since maintaining physical and mental health is an ongoing process, you'll find this oil useful for anointing candles for healing and health issues. In combination with the oil in your spell work, you can use green candles for physical maladies, blue for mental and psychological challenges, and red for sexual organs or fertility issues. Feel free to anoint yourself or another person, as this oil is safe for the skin, as well as spell papers for use in other spells and objects like stones or amulets that you carry regularly. Here, patchouli and thyme promote physical health and healing, while marjoram brings protection from physical maladies. It also includes puri-fying anise, anxiety-easing lavender, and slippery elm to promote mental stability. Stones contribute their own magic, including bloodstone for healing and blood issues, garnet for healing and protection, and red jasper for stress, sexual health, and circulation.

**Glass bottle with cork or lid, in a size of your choosing**

**Base oil: grapeseed oil, olive oil, or vegetable oil**

**Herbs (as many as you choose): patchouli, thyme,**

**marjoram, anise, lavender, slippery elm**

**Stones (as many as you choose): bloodstone, garnet, or red jasper**

1. Fill a glass bottle not quite to the top with your base oil, leaving some space for other ingredients.

2. Add the herbs.

3. Add a stone to your oil—a small chip will do if you're making a small bottle.

4. Leave your bottle of healing oil under the light of a full moon to charge it. After that, it's ready to use. Never let your bottle go empty; keep adding your base oil and other ingredients as needed and desired.

# To Ease Anxiety and Fear Before Medical Procedures

Preparation for a medical procedure can be laced with anxiety, trepidation, and fear. We rightfully place a lot of trust and confidence in the health care workers that help us through difficult times. Let's help them out with a little magical push to encourage a positive outcome. This spell uses green moss agate to encourage positive healing energy, and the stone can be easily carried along to the procedure, while the sandalwood incense aids cleansing.

**Charcoal briquette (the kind that's safe to burn indoors, found at new-age shops or candle and incense shops)**

**Cauldron or fireproof receptacle**

**Matches**

**Green pillar candle**

**Sandalwood incense**

**Stone: green moss agate**

**Table and chair**

**Scissors**

**Paper and pen**

1. Light the charcoal briquette in your cauldron or fireproof receptacle.

2. Light the candle and incense and place the green moss agate near the base of the candle.

3. While your briquette is heating up, seat yourself at a table and cut a sheet of paper into several small slips. On each one, write an affirmation, such as *My procedure will be successful*; *I won't experience any complications*; *I will heal quickly*; and *I won't be afraid*. Add to this list whatever else comes to mind for your needs.

4. One by one, lay each slip of paper on top of the hot charcoal and allow it to burn to ash.

*Continued*

5. When the ashes have all cooled, gather them and toss them into the wind, sending your positive affirmations out into the universe.

6. Extinguish your candle and incense.

7. Keep the stone with you while you wait for your procedure by carrying it in your pocket or keeping it in your purse, and pack it in your bag so it goes with you on the big day.

8. Post-procedure, you can hold this healing stone in your hand for comfort and to absorb the healing energy.

# Healing from a Broken Relationship

Not all relationships are meant to last forever, and when a relationship ends, it's not always a bad thing. Still, it's a painful experience. This spell utilizes sage to support cleansing and purification and is meant to help you move on, heal, and progress toward new, healthy connections. It's important to note that it's meant to be cast *after* the relationship has ended and the people involved have physically parted ways.

**Large trash bag**

**Mementos from your ended relationship (photos, clothing, gifts, and so on)**

**Paper and pen**

**Sage bundle**

**Matches**

1. First, gather up all mementos from this relationship that may be left over in your home, whether photos, a piece of clothing, gifts you received, or a random item. What do you feel you need to hang on to as a keepsake? Anything? Make an honest choice.

2. Put all the items you're not going to keep in a large trash bag.

3. Sit down and write a letter to your former partner. Write down what you may have already said, what you forgot to say, and what you wish you had said. If there is a third party involved, write them a letter, as well.

4. Add these items to the trash bag.

5. Take the bag with you on a drive. Drive as long and as far as you feel you need to; the seclusion of a solitary drive is the perfect time to think and reflect. When you feel the time is right, dispose of the bag. You'll find that most public parks have trash bins, and you can dispose of your bag in a responsible manner.

6. If going for a drive is not possible, find a quiet, solitary spot so you have time to think and reflect on the situation. When you feel ready, take the bag to your trash and toss it.

7. Follow through by saging yourself, your home, and your vehicle.

# Attracting Couple's Harmony

This is a spell performed over several evenings and designed to enhance and build upon an existing relationship. Should you so choose, you and your partner can work this spell together. Use figure candles that reflect your personal relationship and genders, as well as rose petals for romantic love and passion. Some Wiccans keep a "disposable" tarot deck for the express purpose of using the cards in spell work, and you may choose to enhance this spell by using The Lovers card. Be prepared to devote the time; the results will be worth your efforts.

**2 figure candles**

**Large plate or tray**

**Crushed rose petals**

**Matches**

**12 to 14 inches of red ribbon**

**The Lovers tarot card (optional)**

1. Place one figure candle to represent yourself and one to represent your partner on either side of a large plate or tray.

2. Between the figures, place a line of crushed rose petals.

3. Each evening, light the candles. Move them closer to each other every night, allowing them to burn for about five minutes. The number of nights you will do this depends upon how fast your candles burn down.

4. If you're doing this spell together as a couple, on every evening, hold hands. First, meditate thoughtfully on what you love about each other. Then each partner will tell the other two things that they love about them.

5. If you're working the spell alone, meditate thoughtfully on what you love about your partner.

6. On the last evening, make sure the candles have met in the middle of the plate and that they are touching. Allow them to burn for five minutes.

7. Tie the two candles together—with The Lovers card, if you choose—with a red ribbon and keep them beneath your bed. This can be a permanent spot for your candles, or you can bury them on consecrated ground such as in a cemetery, in a garden, or beneath a tree.

# Attracting Harmony to the Home

White sage is burned to cleanse and purify a space. Sometimes creating harmony in a space is as simple as keeping it saged and cleansed so that negative energy and lower-form entities (known as demons in some traditions) won't fester and cause problems. On a monthly basis, sage your home, ideally on the dark moon of each month.

| | |
|---|---|
| **White sage bundle** | **Matches** |
| **White pillar candle** | |

1. Crack open a window or windows.

2. Light your sage bundle and a white pillar candle and begin in the rooms on the lowest floor.

3. Enter each room and move around it deosil (clockwise), stating out loud your intentions of clearing the space of all negative energy. Demand that it leaves. Claim your space, saying, *This space is sacred and my own; I claim this space as mine alone.*

4. Move up to the next floor and walk the rooms there, and so on until you're on the top floor.

5. When you've finished the final room, extinguish your candle and sage bundle.

6. Close your window(s).

## CHAPTER 7

# Spells to Encourage and Energize

Sometimes life throws us an unexpected curveball, and we must dig a little deeper within ourselves for encouragement and moral support. Wiccans of all experience levels know that finding the right frame of mind to cast a spell is as imperative to magical success as is solid basic knowledge of herbs, candles, oils, and such. But how does a Wiccan find inspiration to raise power for a successful magical endeavor? The following spells will help you to do just that, setting you on the road to successful spell casting.

# Setting Your Intention

In desperate times, it's often difficult to see the light at the end of the tunnel, but as a beginning Wiccan, you will have to do just that in order to manifest positive change. The idea here is learning how to focus on positive energy, learning how to place trust in your personal ability, and discovering the deeper sense of resolve that often lies just below the surface. To set your intentions for this type of spell work, you're going to have to go deep within, often to those dark and cobwebbed corners of the mind.

To fix your intentions for these spells, consider first spending some time in meditation holding an object connected to your intention. You can also write yourself a letter with all the reasons you need to be focused or pull some tarot cards for a deeper look with much-needed magical clarity.

# A Spell for Fast Manifestation

Sometimes, even in magic, speed is a priority. When something needs to be done, and it needs to be done fast, this spell will come in handy. It can be incorporated with any other spell in order to speed a process along: Perform this one first, then cast the other. Within this spell work, ginger is used for speed, and dragon's blood incense adds potency.

**Red votive candle**

**Base oil: olive oil, grapeseed oil, or vegetable oil**

**Powdered ginger**

**Table or countertop**

**Paper and pen**

**Fireproof plate**

**Incense: dragon's blood**

**Matches**

1. Anoint a red candle with a base oil. Sprinkle a line of powdered ginger on a smooth surface, such as a table or a countertop, and roll the oiled candle in the ginger, pressing gently to ensure the powdered ginger will adhere to the candle.

2. Create a spell paper, writing exactly what it is that needs to hurry up and happen. Fold this paper into a square and place it beneath a fireproof plate.

3. Place the candle on the fireproof plate. Light it and the incense.

4. Allow the candle to burn down, and be sure that you keep an eye on it—when candles are rolled in herbs in this manner, sometimes they burn up very quickly and impressively.

5. Remove the paper from beneath the plate and tear it up into tiny pieces. You can do several things with the pieces: toss them into the wind, release them from a car window as you're whooshing along during a drive, or flush them, sending them unceremoniously on their way.

# A Spell to Spark Self-Confidence

Sometimes we may feel that some dreams are unattainable because we lack the self-confidence to see our own worth and realize our success. Are there goals that you aspire to but hesitate to reach for, afraid of setting the bar too high? With this spell, you will create a manifestation board to help inspire yourself to achieve those goals.

**Pen and paper**

**Scissors**

**Glue**

**White poster board**

**Nail or tack**

**Images from magazines or the Internet**

**White candles: tealight, votive, pillar, or taper (optional)**

**Incense of your choice (optional)**

**Matches (optional)**

**Physical objects connected to your goals (optional)**

1. First, sit down and make a list of your goals, dividing your paper into a square for each goal. What is it you aspire to? What do you want to accomplish? What are your dreams?

2. Cut these squares out and glue them to a large white poster board, leaving space around each square.

3. Hang this board somewhere you'll see it every day.

4. As you come across them in magazines or online, cut out or print images that connect with your goals. Paste these images beside the corresponding goal on your manifestation board.

5. Another option is to hang your manifestation board above a table or shelf where you can place and light candles and incense or set physical objects to connect with your goals and aspirations.

6. Consider your manifestation board an ongoing project because we are always growing and transitioning, and there will always be new goals to set and new dreams to follow.

# To Strengthen Your Willpower

Whether it's something you want to do, something you need to overcome, or something needed for personal growth, this spell will provide you with the magical energy to maintain your supreme strength of willpower and carry on. You're going to use nag champa incense for clarity and sea salt for purification to consecrate an amulet. Once the magic is complete, you'll wear the amulet as a constant personal reminder to stay determined and resolved. Your amulet can be a religious medal that resonates with your spiritual beliefs and practices, a birthstone or your astrological stone, a family keepsake, or some unique design you pick up at a jewelry shop that simply speaks to you.

**Amulet of your choosing**

**Table**

**White pillar candle**

**Incense: nag champa**

**Fireproof plate**

**Matches**

**Small bowl of coarse sea salt**

**Small bowl of water**

1. Place the amulet on a table.

2. Set the candle and incense on a fireproof plate and light them.

3. Place the bowls of sea salt and water near this plate.

4. When you're ready to begin, pick up your amulet and hold it above the bowl of sea salt. Take a pinch of salt and drop it over the amulet while saying, *By the power of earth, I consecrate this amulet for physical strength.*

5. Hold the amulet in the smoke of the incense while saying, *By the power of air, I consecrate this amulet for mental strength.*

6. Hold the amulet above the small bowl of water. Dip the fingers of one hand in the bowl and sprinkle the water over the amulet while saying, *By the power of water, I consecrate this amulet for emotional strength and heightened psychic ability.*

*Continued*

7. Holding the amulet in one hand, pick up the burning candle with the other. Circle the candle over the top of the amulet—deosil to bring something to you or widdershins to banish something from you—while saying, *By the power of fire, I consecrate this amulet for strength of will and passion.*

# To Find a Resolution

This is a spell to help you decide the right course of action for any situation that may come along. Sometimes we just don't have enough self-confidence in our own decisions, or we fear making the wrong choice. When this is the case, you can turn to this spell to show you the way, provide food for thought, or come straight to the point with an answer.

Paper and pen

Black taper candle

A thoughtfully chosen essential oil:

> Rose oil for issues of love
>
> Patchouli oil for issues of the body

Mint oil for issues of money and finance

Rosemary oil for life's big decisions

6 straight pins

Candleholder

Matches

1. On a sheet of paper, draw a large circle and divide it into pieces, much like a pie. The number of sections you make will depend on the number of possibilities you're looking at. You may also find it useful to leave one section blank in case there's a possibility that hasn't made itself known yet.

2. Within each section, write down a possible solution to your dilemma or situation.

3. Anoint the taper candle with your chosen essential oil and insert six pins halfway up the candle, around the entire candle's circumference. Place the candle in a holder and set it in the center of the circle.

4. Light the candle. When the first pin falls, watch what section it lands on and read what you've written in that space. This will be the answer you're looking for.

## To See the Truth

Whether because of a foggy perception or a desire to believe someone even though our intuition tells us otherwise, it's often difficult to see the truth, even when it's right in front of us. Cast in the bathroom, where a mirror can be easily fogged, this is a spell to help us see more clearly.

**Paper and pen**                         **Matches**

**Red votive candle**                     **Small hand mirror**

**Fireproof plate**

1. Close the bathroom door and turn your shower or bathtub tap on hot, letting the room fill with steam.

2. On a piece of paper write, *As the fog descends, the truth grows near. As the mirror clears, the truth is here.*

3. Place a red votive candle on a fireproof plate.

4. Fold the paper three times and place it beneath the candle.

5. Light the candle.

6. Seat yourself on the floor with your mirror in hand. Watch the mirror and notice when it begins to fog over. Once it is completely covered, take the mirror outside the bathroom and allow it to clear. Snuff out the candle before leaving the room.

7. As the mirror clears, the truth will be revealed to you.

# To Energize a Relationship

With this spell, you'll encourage some extra enthusiasm and excitement within your relationship. While it's not that relationships get boring, people often get in a rut. Though comfortable, ruts are not always exciting. Let some magical spark into your partnership, if you like!

**10 to 20 sparklers**

**Red pillar candle**

**Fireproof plate**

**Matches**

1. Find a clear outdoor spot, preferably a semiprivate area like a garden, backyard, or wild spot away from prying eyes.

2. Create a circle large enough for you to fit inside, using sparklers around the perimeter. Stick the sparklers in the ground, spaced evenly, all the way around you. Ensure there are no leaves or twigs nearby that could present a fire hazard.

3. Light the red pillar candle inside the circle and set it on a fireproof plate. Place this plate at the southern compass point for the element of fire.

4. Beginning at the north end of your circle, light the sparklers one after the other, working your way all around the circle.

5. When they're all lit, dance and chant from the center of the circle, saying, *There's a spark of life to both our hearts, exploding in passion, and love, and fresh new starts.*

6. When the sparklers have died out, the candle has burned down, or you're all danced out, clear the mess. Prepare a special surprise for your sweetheart this evening, whether it's a favorite meal, a night on the town, or a bubble bath and an intimate evening.

# To Encourage and Magnify
# Your Personal Power

One way we can gain control and confidence over a foe or a difficult situation is by magnifying our own personal power. Sometimes we discover that the giant ogre we think we're facing is in fact a timid mouse in disguise. This spell will help you deal with that mouse. Depending on your particular needs, use sandalwood for cleansing and purification, nag champa to add clarity, or dragon's blood to provide strength, protection, and boundaries.

**Paper and a pen**

**Fireproof plate**

**Magnifying glass**

**3 red votive candles**

**Matches**

**Incense of your choice, such as sandalwood, nag champa, or dragon's blood**

**Large red cotton or velvet bag**

1. On a sheet of paper, write a list of what it is you feel you're up against. On the other side of the paper, write down all the attributes you think you need to overcome this situation or to overpower this individual.

2. Fold the paper three times and place it on a fireproof plate.

3. On top of the paper, lay a magnifying glass.

4. Place three red candles around the magnifying glass.

5. Light the candles and incense.

6. Allow the candles to burn down.

7. Gather the remains of the candles, the spell paper, and the magnifying glass and add them to a large red cotton or velvet bag. Tie this bag shut and keep it somewhere safe, such as your closet or a desk drawer. It may be kept indefinitely, working in the background for your benefit. If you feel the need to dispose of it, do so by dismantling the remains of the bag and burying the items separately beneath a tree or near a body of water.

# To Encourage Creativity

This range of simple spells will help you find your muse and reconnect with your creative magic. Muses are goddesses of creativity and the arts, and it's their inspiration that drives the writers, poets, painters, artists, and anyone who needs their unique encouragement. Think of your muse like a guardian angel—one who brings not protection but the spark of creative adventure. What will spark your muse? Experiment with a variety of easy magical triggers and discover what works for you and your inspirational goddess.

**Yellow candle: tealight, votive, pillar, or taper**

**Matches**

**Table and chair**

**Notebook or journal and pen**

**Tea bag of your choice**

**Teacup**

**Ice cube**

**Heating pad**

**Bathtub and favorite bubble bath soap**

**Fireplace and wood**

1. **Light a yellow candle** for creations of communication, such as writing, whether it's music, poetry, or prose, or any art form. Seat yourself near the candle and scry (see Crystal Ball and Scrying Mirror on page 50 to find out how) the flame for information and inspiration.

2. **Write a journal entry** addressing your muse as though she were a real person seated before you. What will you say to her? What will you ask of her? What will you confide in her?

3. **Cue your muse** that you're ready to create by fixing yourself a cup of special tea, perhaps a blend that you reserve and drink for this purpose alone.

4. **Summon your muse in summer** with ice. Hold an ice cube in your hand until you feel it start to melt or until the cold becomes too much for your hand and you must drop it.

*Continued*

5. **Summon your muse in winter** with heat. Perhaps place a heating pad against the back of your desk chair where you write, take a hot bath, or light up the fireplace if you have one, or a pillar candle if you do not. Meditate by the flame and await the inspiration.

## CHAPTER 8

# Spells for Friends and Family

The Wiccan is legendary for looking after their kith and kin. For many Wiccan practitioners, one of the most important aspects of their spell craft is the ability to take care of their loved ones. These spells are designed to work magic in the lives of those around us, like our most cherished friends and family members.

# Setting Your Intention

Getting your emotions to run energetically high is not going to be a prob-lem when it comes to casting spells for those closest to you. You want the people most important to you to be healthy, happy, and safe. There's nothing that will raise your energy faster, or make your magic more power-ful, than to know that a friend or family member is in need of serious help. To aid your focus, consider meditating on your intention while holding a photo of a family member or an item connected to them. You may want to consult your tarot cards for added insight or even have tea, if possible, with the subject of your spell for an extra connection and added focus.

# A Family Blessing

Designed to bless a family (or chosen family) dynamic and help its members appreciate each other, this spell incorporates hibiscus for love, passion, and positive emotions; pink roses to amplify affection and friendship; red geraniums to encourage strong feelings of love; white geraniums for purity of intention; yellow marigolds to enhance clear and open communication; and lavender to bring peaceful energy.

**Large bowl**

**Herbs: hibiscus, pink roses, red geraniums, white geraniums, yellow marigolds**

**Essential oil: lavender**

**Paper and pen**

**Pink votive candle**

**Incense: rose or lavender**

**Matches**

**Fireproof container**

1. On a full-moon night, in a large bowl, combine the flower blossoms.

2. Add a sprinkling of lavender oil.

3. On a sheet of paper, write down the names of all the inhabitants in your household or in the house for which this bowl is destined.

4. Fold the paper up and place it beneath the bowl, leaving it to sit for about an hour.

5. Light a pink candle and the incense.

6. Light the name paper on fire and drop it into the fireproof container to burn to ash. Dispose of the ashes as you choose, such as by scattering them to the wind or putting them in the trash.

7. Take the bowl of flowers to the threshold of the front door and sprinkle them about the porch, the stairway if there is one, and the front walkway.

8. As the inhabitants walk over the blossoms, the energy of love and devotion, friendship, positive communication, peace and calm, loyalty, and passion will fill their hearts.

# Smoothing Marital Turmoil

The emotional tenor of your relationship with your significant other can affect your life to its core, especially when things get tempestuous. This spell to smooth rough waters utilizes rose quartz for affectionate love, blue lace agate to enhance peaceful emotions, and clear quartz crystal to energize. While this spell was created for married people experiencing a hiccup, it can easily be cast on their behalf by a family member or close friend. A word of warning: If you're considering casting this spell for someone else, use discretion and caution. No one truly understands the dynamics of a marriage other than those individuals involved, and sometimes interference from well-meaning family or friends is not desired.

**Paper and pen**

**Bathroom sink**

**Stones: rose quartz, blue lace agate, clear quartz crystal**

**White velvet or cotton bag**

1. On a small piece of paper, write down what is causing the problem.

2. Plug your bathroom sink and fill it half full of water.

3. In the sink place the three stones.

4. Drop the slip of paper into the water.

5. With both hands, agitate the water to shake it up and make it splash. As you do this, say, *Rough waters be gone and done; my true love and I unite as one.*

6. If you are casting this spell for a friend or family member, say, *Rough waters be gone and done; this couple needs to unite as one.*

7. Stop agitating the water and allow it to become perfectly still.

8. Retrieve the stones and place them in a white velvet or cotton bag. Keep the bag close: in your nightstand, beneath your bed, or in a place that's special for you. If you've worked this spell for friends, give it to them to keep close, ideally in their bedroom.

# Straightening Out a Misunderstanding

Some misunderstandings are a cluster of miscommunications: information coming from well-meaning but secondhand sources, or our own misinterpretation of someone's motives, actions, or intentions. Cast this spell to smooth out the wrinkles, using rose for love and passion or jasmine to support a less physical love and more peaceful emotions, as well as clear quartz crystal for clarity.

**Cloth handkerchief**

**Black velvet or cotton bag**

**Pink votive candle**

**Essential oil: rose or jasmine**

**Fireproof plate**

**Matches**

**Incense: rose or jasmine**

**Ironing board or heavy bath towel**

**Iron**

**Stone: clear quartz crystal**

1. A day or two before you cast this spell, take a cloth handkerchief and slightly dampen it. Crush it into a ball and place it in a black velvet or cotton bag and let it sit.

2. On the day you cast this spell, anoint a pink candle with oil and place it on a fireproof plate. Light the candle and incense.

3. Set up your ironing board or, if you don't have one, double up a towel and place it on a table or countertop to serve the same purpose.

4. Plug in your iron and let it heat up.

5. Retrieve the handkerchief from the black bag.

6. Take up your iron and iron the wrinkles out of the handkerchief, all the while chanting, *As these wrinkles disappear, feelings and motives become crystal clear.*

7. Fold the handkerchief neatly, tuck it in a dresser drawer, and set a clear crystal stone on top of it. The handkerchief may be kept in this spot indefinitely, or until the misunderstanding has cleared.

# A Spell for a Healthy Baby

Pregnancy can be one of the happiest times in a person's life, but it can also be a stressful time, particularly if there are medical issues. Even just the anxiety that comes from knowing that a new human being is on the horizon and wanting everything to be perfect for their arrival can cause stress. Whether you and your partner are expecting or a family member or close friend is going through this experience, use this spell to raise healthy energy for a healthy baby. The sandalwood included here offers cleansing, purification, and healthy energy.

**Table and chair**

**White pillar candle**

**Incense: sandalwood**

**Matches**

**9 feet of white ribbon or cord**

**White velvet or cotton bag**

1. Seat yourself somewhere comfortably, either at a table or in your favorite chair.

2. Light the white candle and incense.

3. Tie a knot at one end of the white ribbon or cord. Tie a second knot at the other end. Between these two knots, tie seven more.

4. While you tie these knots, chant, *A healthy baby there will be, by the awesome power of three times three.*

5. Place this ribbon in a white velvet or cotton bag and keep it in a safe place until the time of delivery draws near.

6. Once labor has begun, undo the knots and release the magic.

# Planting the Seed: A Spell to Encourage Fertility

This spell is for couples to use in conjunction with their physician or fertility specialist, who work their own scientific magic with knowledge and treatments. However, a little magic to boost Mother Nature's part never hurts. In this encouraging spell, flower seeds and stones work together to support fertility. Bachelor's buttons add healthy, happy energy and fertility, while forget-me-nots work to fulfill wishes and dreams. Sodalite supports intuition and dreams, lapis offers second sight and abundance, pink tourmaline and rose quartz contribute love and affection, and rhodochrosite warms the heart. This is also a spell the family can use for a couple who needs some additional magical help and encouragement getting their family started.

**7 small flowerpots**

**7 blue stones: sodalite or lapis**

**7 pink stones: rose quartz, rhodochrosite, or pink tourmaline**

**7 clear quartz crystal points (optional)**

**Potting soil**

**Flower seeds: pink bachelor's buttons, forget-me-nots**

**Paper and pen**

**White pillar candle**

**Matches**

**White velvet or cotton bag**

1. In the bottom of seven small flowerpots, place two stones each, a blue one and a pink one. If you'd like the sex of an unborn child to remain nature's secret, place a clear quartz crystal point in the flowerpot instead of the blue and pink stones.

2. Fill the pots with potting soil.

3. To each flowerpot, add six seeds: three seeds for blue flowers and three seeds for pink flowers.

*Continued*

# Planting the Seed: A Spell to Encourage Fertility CONTINUED

4. On a sheet of paper, write down several names you've been thinking about for girls and boys. Include at least four to six names for each sex, including gender-neutral names.

5. Fold this paper up and place it beneath one of the flowerpots.

6. Every night for seven nights, light the white candle amid the flowerpots and allow it to burn for 5 to 10 minutes.

7. On the seventh night, take the slip of paper from beneath the flowerpot and place it in a white velvet or cotton bag. Keep this bag in a safe place, such as a dresser drawer or a jewelry box.

8. Continue to water the pots, nurture the flowers, and enjoy their gentle growth.

9. The universe hears you. Allow it time to work—anywhere from one to two years. There is a soul out there who needs to be born, and the universe will connect them with the right family.

# A Magical Adoption

For those who decide that adoption is the best route for them, this spell will put a blessing from Spirit on your endeavors. The true magic will happen the first time you look into the eyes of the child that's meant for you. This spell, a magical manifestation board, can also be used by the friends and family of a couple who are taking this journey in order to provide them with the magical energy they'll need. Rosemary is utilized for cleansing and clarity, rose adds loving energy, sandalwood brings purity of intentions, and clear quartz crystals provide energizing and purification.

**Images of children, from magazines or computer printouts**

**Scissors**

**Glue**

**White poster board**

**Pen or marker**

**3 votive candles: white,**

**pink, and blue**

**Essential oil: rosemary, rose, or sandalwood**

**Matches**

**White velvet or cotton bag**

**Stones: 3 clear quartz crystals**

**Tack**

1. Start by collecting truly diverse images of children, and in ages ranging from infants to older children. This collection should also be based on your own expectations; just remember that Spirit can some-times bring to us someone completely unexpected that turns out to be a profound blessing.

2. Cut out these images and start pasting them on a large white poster board.

3. Keep a pen or marker handy. You can write on this board what-ever your heart feels, such as names, anticipations, fears, desires, or dreams.

*Continued*

4. On the night before a full moon, anoint the three candles with essential oil and light them, saying, *By the grace of Spirit, make my intentions clear; open a path for my child to come to me; as I do will, so mote it be.*

5. In a white velvet or cotton bag, place the quartz crystals and any wax remaining from the candles.

6. Tack this bag to your manifestation board. Periodically, either on specific moon phases or at times when it calls to your heart, visit the board. Close your eyes for a few moments of meditation and feel the energy.

# Jar of Inspiration: A Spell for Strength to the Caretaker

This spell is for the caretaker of a loved one with any kind of chronic condition. It's a hug from Spirit to instill strength, peace, and optimism. This spell, which uses many herbs and stones in conjunction, may be cast by the caregiver themselves or on their behalf by a friend or family member. Marjoram brings love, strength, and healing; St. John's wort adds stamina and strength; thyme adds healing; eyebright brings clarity; rosemary supports cleansing; mint offers health and protection; anise encourages purification; lavender delivers peace and calm; sage brings purification; chamomile is for calm, peaceful energy; and peppermint helps clear the air of negativity. Stones round out the magic, including chalcedony for peaceful energy, kunzite for inspiration and to relieve anxiety, and lepidolite for mental health and stability.

**Paper and pen**

**Quart mason jar with lid**

**Herbs: marjoram, St. John's wort, thyme, eyebright, rosemary, mint, anise,** **lavender, sage**

**Stones: chalcedony, kunzite, lepidolite**

**Essential oil: lavender, chamomile, peppermint**

1. Begin by writing the name of the caregiver on a slip of paper, then place it in the mason jar.

2. Add the herbs and stones to the jar.

3. Add three drops of each of the essential oils.

*Continued*

## Jar of Inspiration: A Spell for Strength to the Caretaker
CONTINUED

4. As you cap this jar, say, *As I nurse your body, I hold your heart to mine. As I calm your spirit, I soothe your troubled soul. As you take this journey, we travel together. When you pass through the veil, I know you will light the way for me.*

5. Keep this jar in a spot where it will be seen every day and become part of the household, warming the energy of the home and the hearts of those who live there.

# A Family Reunion Blessing: A Spell to Ensure a Successful Gathering

Some of us have fond childhood memories of family reunions. We all know that real life isn't always this way, but this spell will help you unite your family (or chosen family) in a magical way that's filled with positive energy and memories, if only for a day. It utilizes chamomile to bring serenity; rosemary for purification and stable energy; sage to support purification and protection from negative energy; lavender to add peaceful, loving vibes; and sea salt for purification.

**Bag of small river rocks**

**Black marker**

**Large bucket or pail**

**Hammer and nail (optional)**

**Coarse sea salt**

**Herbs: chamomile, rosemary, sage, lavender**

**Potting soil**

**Wildflower seeds**

1. A reunion usually means lots of people. Take inventory about four weeks before the planned event, and as you do, record each person's name on a small rock with a black marker and place it in the pail.

2. Use a hammer and nail to punch holes in the bottom of the pail for drainage, if you choose.

3. Sprinkle a very small pinch of coarse sea salt into the pail over the rocks, along with the herbs.

4. Fill the remainder of the pail with potting soil.

5. Generously sprinkle the mixed wildflower seeds over the top of the soil.

6. Water and nurture this pail of potential wildflowers up to the date of your reunion.

7. When you pack the car with all the good food and libations to go to the reunion, don't forget the reunion pail. It's going with you, and so is its energy for a happy family.

# Magical Moves: A Spell to Help Ease Anxiety During Relocation

Relocating, while exciting and adventurous, can also be a time of high anxiety and stress. Intended to help you along this journey, this lucky penny jar spell includes plantain to ensure safe travels and good health, calamus for safe travel, lavender to encourage peaceful energy, chamomile to ease anxiety, rosemary to cleanse, and sage to purify and protect. It also utilizes stones, including turquoise for safe travel and protection, dalmatian jasper for safe travel, aventurine for health and prosperity, jade for peaceful energy, and prehnite for peaceful energy and mental clarity.

**Scissors**

**Paper and pen**

**Quart mason jar and lid**

**Herbs: plantain, calamus, lavender, chamomile, rosemary, sage**

**Stones: turquoise, dalmatian jasper, aventurine, jade, prehnite**

**Pennies (the amount will depend on how long before your move you begin this project)**

1. Cut small strips of paper and write down the questions and anxieties that you have about the process of relocation, such as *Will we find a new dwelling that fits our needs? Will we be able to stay in budget? Will our old house sell for a good price?* and *Will family and friends be okay with our move?*

2. Add these papers to the mason jar.

3. Add the herbs and stones to the jar.

4. Cap the jar and set it where it's in plain sight and easily accessible.

5. Every three days before your relocation, add a penny to the jar. When you're ready to hit the road, make sure the jar goes with you. When you arrive at your new home, carry forward the energy of this jar and find a place of honor to put it. Your lucky penny jar is now a family keepsake and a reminder of life's adventures.

## CHAPTER 9

# Spells for Gratitude, Abundance, and Success

To make life happy and complete, even the most humble and frugal among us need abundance. Success can assure us that these needs will be met. The spells in this chapter are not about attaining vast wealth but rather about bringing us what we need to live happily and comfortably in this world. Each person's definition of success is unique and highly personalized, so think about what it is that brings you gratitude and a sense of prosperity.

# Setting Your Intention

To set intentions for spells of prosperity and abundance, we have to get over the guilt that may be instilled in us when it comes to casting spells for personal gain. Contrary to popular misinformation, it is perfectly okay to cast spells that will benefit you personally. You use magic to take care of the world and its people; why wouldn't you cast a spell to take care of yourself? Clear your mind, ground and center, and know that you have the blessing of Spirit for this magic.

If it is funds you need for a particular purpose, find ways to connect with this purpose through pictures or objects relating to it. Meditate on the purpose itself, the reason behind your present need and your desire to cast a spell like this. If you are striving toward a goal of accomplishment, set yourself up with visual images as reminders of what you're working toward. Meditate and focus on positive energy; *know* you can do what you set your mind to.

# Prosperity Oil

This is a magical oil that can be used with any money or prosperity spell to anoint spell candles, spell papers, stones, talismans, amulets, and such. As with all magical oils, never let the bottle run empty—continue adding a base oil, as well as other ingredients, as needed. With all magical oils, it seems the older they get, the stronger their potency becomes. My bottle of prosperity oil was created over a decade ago and is still lending its energy to my spells. Within this spell, you'll utilize mint and cinnamon to draw money; patchouli to encourage physical abundance, prosperity, and manifestation; allspice to bring wealth; and peppermint to fuel abundance and high energy.

**Bottle in the size and style of your choosing, with lid or cap**

**Base oil: olive oil, grapeseed oil, or vegetable oil**

**Herbs: dried mint, cinnamon stick, dried patchouli, whole allspice**

**Essential oil: peppermint or patchouli**

1. Fill the bottle almost to the top with your base oil, leaving enough room for the herbs.

2. Add the herbs and several drops of essential oil.

3. Cap your bottle.

4. You can allow your prosperity oil to sit out under the light of a full moon to charge it. Keep it in a safe place, and shake it up before you use it.

# A Money Charm

With this potent spell, you'll create a money charm that you can tuck in your purse or wallet or wear as a pendant. If you're going to be wearing a pendant, choose any design that appeals to you. If you're going to create an amulet, you can also choose whatever you wish, of course, but it would be beneficial if it were symbolic of money and prosperity, such as a metal money clip, a special coin, or another object that you connect with material forms of abundance. Patchouli is used to enhance the physical manifestation of your abundance desires.

**Green pillar or votive candle**

**Prosperity Oil (page 133)**

**Matches**

**Incense: patchouli**

**Pendant or object for an amulet**

**For a pendant: silver chain or black cord (optional)**

**For an amulet: green velvet or cotton bag, dried mint and patchouli, aventurine stone (optional)**

1. Anoint a green candle with prosperity oil. Light the candle, then light the incense.

2. Anoint your chosen pendant or amulet with prosperity oil.

3. If you'll be wearing a pendant, put it on a chain or a cord and pass it through the smoke of the incense. As you do so, know that your pendant is charged and the energy is ready to work for you.

4. If you're anointing an amulet, add it to a green bag along with a pinch of mint and patchouli and the aventurine. Pass the bag through the smoke of the incense. Carry this bag in your purse or on your person, or keep it in a safe place in your home indefinitely.

5. You can recharge the charm by anointing it with a drop of prosperity oil, or you can recharge and refresh the energy by leaving the pendant or bag overnight in the light of a full moon. You can even do both, making for some supercharged and potent prosperity energy.

# Growing a Pot of Wealth

Mint is the magical herb that's the most popular for prosperity and money spells, and there's nothing like growing your own to draw this energy to you. With this spell, it's time to do some simple container gardening and call upon your magical green thumb. In addition to mint, this spell includes aventurine to encourage wealth and physical manifestation, moss agate to bring abundance, and malachite to deliver intense, busy energy and movement. Mint is so easy to grow from a cutting and so abundant a plant unto itself that there's no need to buy seeds if you have access to an existing plant.

**Flowerpot**

**Coins: 1 quarter, 1 nickel, 1 dime, 1 penny**

**Stone: aventurine, moss agate, or malachite**

**Potting soil**

**Mint seeds or cutting**

1. Choose a container that appeals to you and is the right size for the space you'll keep your plant.

2. In the bottom of the flowerpot, place the four coins.

3. Add the green stone of your choice.

4. Fill the pot with potting soil, leaving enough room to add your seeds or cutting.

5. Plant your seeds or transplant your young mint.

6. Water and nurture this plant with loving care; it's working to bring you prosperity and wealth.

# A Bowl of Abundance

This is a spell to make sure that your house never runs dry of funds, whether money to pay for your necessities or to cover bills. You're going to create a bowl of abundance to sit on top of the refrigerator or a bookshelf—someplace where it won't be disturbed. This spell requires an *open* safety pin, the traditional addition to this magical bowl to keep the lines of abundance open. However, you can use any kind of pin that opens and closes, or even something personal, such as a favorite brooch. The spell uses rice to bring abundance, sea salt to encourage purity of intentions and a connection to the earth element, mint to deliver money and abundance, and peppermint for abundance.

Ideally, keep this bowl undisturbed for an indefinite amount of time. If you feel some need to refresh it, you can create a new bowl to take its place, but don't remove the original until the new one is complete.

**Small ceramic bowl**

**Uncooked rice**

**Coarse sea salt**

**Safety pin or brooch**

**Herbs: dried crushed mint (optional)**

**Essential oil: peppermint (optional)**

**Prosperity Oil (page 133) (optional)**

1. Choose a pretty little bowl and put a handful of rice and a handful of coarse sea salt in it.

2. Place a large open safety pin or a brooch in the bowl.

3. You may also add some dried crushed mint, several drops of peppermint essential oil, or a few drops of prosperity oil.

4. Keep this bowl in a safe spot to work its magic, such as in a place of honor on your altar, or a handy spot on a bookshelf. Mine sits on top of the refrigerator.

# A Success Jar

A spell in a jar is another form of a witch's bottle. With this spell, we'll create one for success. You'll choose the elements based on your own concepts of success, filling it with corresponding herbs, stones, and other mundane and magical items. You can keep the jar, bury it, or add to the energy by incorporating items like stones, oil, spell papers, and such. When choosing herbs, keep in mind that patchouli draws prosperity and abundance, calendula (marigold) offers success and heightened intuition, poppy seeds bring abundance, lemon balm and sage support cleansing and safety, hyssop manifests prosperity and success, rosemary fosters peace, and anise inspires heightened intuition and success. Choose three of the following stones, depending upon the aim of your spell: tigereye for victory and safety; turquoise for safety and peace; aventurine for money and abundance; blue kunzite for clarity and peace; clear quartz crystal for clarity, success, and energy; rose quartz for love and peace; and apatite for victory, emotional stability, and intuition.

**Herbs: mint, patchouli, calendula (marigold), poppy seeds, lemon balm, sage, hyssop, rosemary, anise, or star anise**

**Quart mason jar with lid**

**3 of the following stones: tigereye, turquoise, aventurine, blue kunzite,** **clear quartz crystal, rose quartz, or apatite**

**Paper and pen**

**Essential oil: peppermint**

**Mundane or magical items specifically connected to your intentions (optional)**

1. Layer your choice of herbs in the quart mason jar.

2. On top of the herbs, lay the three stones you've chosen.

3. Write your intention on a spell paper. Add the spell paper to the jar and sprinkle in six drops of peppermint oil.

*Continued*

## A Success Jar CONTINUED

4. Add any personal magical or mundane items.

5. You may choose to leave the jar out in the light of the next full moon to charge it. This jar may become a permanent fixture on your magical shelves.

# Being Thankful: A Spell to Pay It Forward

It's said that what you send out, you get back threefold. This spell abides by that truthful prophecy, and what you'll be sending out is gratitude in the guise of generosity. The generosity that you so thoughtfully show toward others will be sent back to you in the reciprocal energy of friends, family, and sometimes strangers. Your spell will utilize mint to bring prosperity and wealth or patchouli to encourage physical manifestation and earth energy, as well as clear quartz crystals to draw energy.

**Green votive candle**

**Essential oil: mint or patchouli**

**Matches**

**Fireproof plate**

**Stones: 3 clear quartz crystals**

**Prosperity Oil (page 133)**

**Green velvet or cotton bag**

1. On the night of a waxing gibbous moon, anoint with essential oil and light a green candle, placing it on a fireproof plate.

2. Anoint three clear quartz crystals with prosperity oil and arrange them around the base of the candle.

3. When the candle has burned down, collect the remains of the candle wax and the three stones and place them in your green bag.

4. Carry this bag in your purse, your wallet, or the glove compartment of your vehicle.

5. On the day that a full moon will rise, visit a coffee shop or a casual restaurant. When you make your purchase, pick up the tab for the person behind you.

# Flying High: A Wild-Bird Gratitude Spell

There are things that we are grateful for every day. Some we take for granted but would notice if they weren't there; others are pleasant surprises sent from Spirit. Think about what it is you're grateful for: a loving family, opportunities to do work that inspires you, good health, a pet that you love, or a special connection that may have turned into a lifelong association. Let's thank the universe and show our gratitude by feeding her flock. Here you'll use rose for loving, enthusiastic energy, as well as rose quartz for peaceful, loving vibes.

| | |
|---|---|
| **Bird feeder or metal bowl** | **White pillar candle** |
| **Bag of birdseed** | **Incense: rose** |
| **7 rose quartz stones** | **Matches** |

1. Set up a bird feeder or a metal bowl in your backyard, on the balcony or fire escape of your apartment, or on your back door stoop; wherever you live, there are birds.

2. Pour birdseed into your feeder or bowl.

3. Around the bird feeder or bowl, place seven stones of rose quartz.

4. Light the candle and incense and meditate by the bird feeder on your life and how fortunate you are. Think of all the things that you have to be grateful for, and think about how grateful the wildlife will be to receive this offering.

5. When you're ready, extinguish the candle and incense and remove them, along with the stones.

6. Retreat so that the wildlife can claim their offering, but watch them from close by if you like.

# Seeds of Abundance

When people talk about prosperity and wealth, they often speak in terms of "planting" and "growth," the same terms that could be used for a garden. With this spell, you're going to plant seeds of abundance, literally, using herbs connected with this energy, including poppy for abundance and dill for abundance and financial security, in addition to moss agate for money and abundance. You can use this spell either outdoors, if you have an actual garden spot, or within flowerpots for an indoor abundant garden.

**Flowerpots, as many as you desire**

**Stones: 1 moss agate for each flowerpot**

**Potting soil**

**Herbs: poppy seeds, dill seeds**

1. Line up your flowerpots and place a moss agate stone in the bottom of each one.

2. Pour in the potting soil, leaving about an inch of space at the top.

3. Add several seeds of each variety to your pots.

4. Water carefully, and nurture them well.

5. Once your plants have grown, you can pinch off a leaf or two from time to time to carry in your purse or wallet or to use in other spells for prosperity and abundance.

**CHAPTER 10**

# Spells for Binding and Protection

Spells for binding (magically tying your enemies' hands to prevent them from harming you) and protection fascinate many people. It might be the mysterious idea of a darker side to magical practice, or it may be because this is the side of witchcraft that is most often portrayed in movies, television, and fiction. It goes without saying that even a witch should look for simple and easy no-one-gets-hurt ways of dealing with difficult people, circumstances, and decisions, but there comes a time when even the most patient of witches will have to use firm magical methods.

# Setting Your Intention

This is probably the easiest form of magic to focus on for strength and purity of intentions. If you feel the need to bind someone's behavior or to cast spells of protection, there has to be a lot of anger or fear behind it. Anger and fear are two of the most powerful emotions to work with. The word of caution here is not to do this type of magic—or *any* magic—while you are caught up in the heat of anger. It tends to lead to rash actions and scattered, frenetic energy. First, calm down, then roll up your sleeves and prepare to do some magical work.

Be very clear about your focus for this type of spell, whether this is a particular individual or a specific action that needs to be bound or stopped altogether. Use the night of a dark moon to set aside meditation time, when you either write out exactly what you're feeling with paper and pen or verbalize your thoughts to the universe in a private setting with a chat.

# Binding Negative Behavior

There are times when an individual's behavior will prove to be detrimental to the welfare of others, and even to themselves. When it comes to this point, a binding is in order. Binding someone means that, to a degree, you have interfered with their ability to take certain harmful actions. Toying with an individual's will is not something to do lightly, and it shouldn't be done until all other methods to resolve the problem have been exhausted. A binding is serious business, so always do it with respect and reverence. Binding uses dragon's blood to activate protection and boundaries, whole black pepper to bring protection, rose thorns to activate defense, cayenne pepper to put the heat on an individual, and chili powder to quiet a nasty voice, as well as onyx to protect and tourmaline to deflect negative energy.

**Incense: dragon's blood**

**Matches**

**Black figure candle**

**Essential oil: dragon's blood**

**Knife or carving tool**

**12 inches of red cord or rope**

**Fireproof plate**

**Herbs: whole black pepper, rose thorns (at least 6), powdered cayenne pepper, chili powder**

**Black stones: onyx, tourmaline**

**Black velvet or cotton bag**

1. Light the incense.
2. Anoint the figure candle with essential oil. Carve the target's name on the candle.
3. Wrap the red cord around the candle, beginning at the bottom and working your way up to the head, until you have just enough left to tie it off.
4. Set the candle on a fireproof plate.
5. Circle the candle with the herbs and black stones.

*Continued*

## Binding Negative Behavior CONTINUED

6. Light the candle and allow it to burn down.

7. Remove the spell remains from the plate and place them in the black bag.

8. Bury this bag on consecrated ground, like a cemetery, or in some solitary, secluded location.

# Protective Boundaries for the Home

The first thing to learn about protection is to keep your borders, your boundaries, secure. Whatever it is that you feel is a threat needs to be kept from intruding onto your property and, thus, from being able to intrude on your person, whether physically, mentally, or spiritually. No matter the nature of the protection, prepare to reinforce your perimeters. Here, you'll use sea salt for purification and sage for purification and protection.

| | |
|---|---|
| Coarse sea salt | Broom |
| 4 small bundles of sage | 1 pentacle amulet or pendant for each entrance to your property |
| 4 small mirrors | |

1. Starting at one corner of your lot—whether your own yard or the ground your apartment complex is on—sprinkle pinches of sea salt around the entire perimeter, ending where you began.

2. In the four corners of your property, bury a small bundle of sage. You can also use the sage this way indoors by concealing it in a corner beneath a rug or under a piece of furniture.

3. At the four compass points of your property—north, east, south, and west—bury a small mirror, facing outward away from your property, to reflect negative energy and intentions. The mirrors may also be used indoors by placing them discreetly on the floor against a wall or behind furniture, with their reflective side facing outward.

4. Keep a broom near your front door to sweep away negative energy.

5. Finally, bury a small pentacle amulet or pendant at the entrance of the front gate, the driveway, the back gate, and other entrances to your propert. You can also use your pendant indoors, if for some reason you're not able to bury it outdoors, by concealing it beneath a welcome mat.

# Protection Against Gossip

Gossip can do irreparable damage to your reputation, ruin relationships, snatch away opportunities, and wreak havoc with your well-being. There are ways to stop this irresponsible behavior, and this spell is one of them. You will use either a raw beef tongue (commonly sold in a grocer's meat department) or a portobello mushroom for this spell. This spell calls upon cloves to stop a gossip, cayenne pepper to put the heat on an individual and their wagging tongue, and eyebright to support healthier communication.

**Photo of the target(s) or a name paper**

**Paper and pen (optional)**

**Raw beef tongue or portobello mushroom**

**Herbs: powdered or dried**

**cloves, cayenne pepper, eyebright**

**2 feet of black cord**

**Black velvet or cotton bag, or a large food-storage bag or plastic shopping bag**

1. If you don't have a photo of your target or targets, write their name(s) on a large sheet of white paper, fold it in half, and fold it in half again.

2. On a raw beef tongue or portobello mushroom, sprinkle the herbs.

3. With a black cord, tie the photos or the folded sheet of paper to the beef tongue or portobello mushroom while saying, *With this cord I bind your lies; with this cord I break your ties.*

4. Place the beef tongue or mushroom in the black bag, resealable storage bag, or plastic shopping bag and put it in your freezer. Keep it there as long as you feel the need. If and when you're ready to remove it, throw it away or bury it.

# Return to Sender: A Spell for Magical Rebuttal

Did someone direct some bad mojo toward you? Do you feel the negative magic that has been sent in your direction? Most people are sensitive enough to pick this up. Even if you don't know for sure where this nasty energy and intention is coming from, it's magically possible to send it back to its source. This spell uses cloves, which return negative energy and magic and halt a nasty tongue, to do just that.

**Black votive candle**

**Essential oil: clove or sage**

**Knife or carving tool**

**Small mirror**

**Fireproof plate**

**Herbs: powdered cloves**

**Matches**

1. Anoint the black candle with the oil and carve these words into it: *Return to sender*.

2. Place a small mirror on a fireproof plate and set the candle on the mirror.

3. Sprinkle the cloves around the candle.

4. Light the candle while saying, *Back to you this magic flows. An eye for an eye, and so it goes.*

5. Allow the candle to burn down, then dispose of the wax remains and the mirror as soon as possible. You can throw them in the trash or bury them in a remote and lonely place.

# Protection from Thieves

There's nothing more unscrupulous than a thief. This little spell uses rose thorns to protect you from thievery, whether it involves material possessions, your feelings of safety and well-being, your ideas, or something else that's precious to you.

**Seven of Swords tarot card (optional)**

**Table or altar**

**Fireproof plate**

**White votive candle**

**Magnet**

**Herbs: rose thorns**

**Broken chain (a part of a jewelry chain will work)**

**Matches**

**Black velvet or cotton bag**

1. If you choose to use it as a focus for your intentions, place a Seven of Swords (The Thief) tarot card on a countertop, a tabletop, or your altar.

2. On a small fireproof plate in front of the card, place the candle.

3. Add to this altar space a magnet, rose thorns, and a piece of broken chain.

4. Light your candle while saying, *Step over this, I dare you, Thief. Your time here will be brief. What's mine is mine, be on your way. A pox to you, I do say.*

5. Place the remains of this spell in a black bag and bury the bag in front of a threshold to your property, whether just inside a front gate or on the ground ahead of your front door.

# Protecting New Relationships from Ex Energy

After a certain age, almost everyone has an ex, perhaps even one who has not cut the cord and moved on. These energies can be intrusive, and equally damaging if your new partner is caught up in a codependent relationship with their ex. If this issue is causing trouble in your life, talk to your partner, identify the problem, and work together to solve it. Everyone needs to move on for a fresh start. In concert with communication, cast this spell, which uses garlic to purify and to keep toxic energy away, oregano to keep destructive influences at bay, sea salt to purify, and sage to cleanse, purify, and purge. Choose your figure candles wisely, for your spell will be worked for as many nights as it takes to burn down the candles.

| | |
|---|---|
| **2 figure candles representing the ex-couple** | **Herbs: powdered garlic, sage, oregano** |
| **Essential oil: sage** | **Coarse sea salt** |
| **Fireproof plate** | **Matches** |
| **White cord or rope to reach across your plate** | **Scissors** |
| | **Black velvet or cotton bag** |

1. Anoint the figure candles with oil and place them on a fireproof plate.

2. Between the two candles, lay the white cord or rope in a straight line with the ends touching the candles.

3. Sprinkle the herbs over the cord.

4. Sprinkle a line of salt over the herbs.

5. Light the candles and allow them to burn for half an hour every night.

6. Once the candles have burned down, cut the cord that was connecting the candles.

7. Place the remains of this spell in a black bag and bury the bag beneath a tree.

# Binding the Bully

Bullies are cowards in disguise, and this is a spell to bind their energy and capacity to hurt people, whether physically, mentally, or emotionally. This spell will call for the purchase of a fashion doll, preferably with the same hair color and sex as your target; inexpensive dolls are available at many stores. You may also choose to create your own doll from craft store supplies or to use something as simple as a clothespin to represent the person. Whichever method you choose, the more detail you add, the better the results will be. While this spell does not replace counselors, therapists, or other protective measures, it can be used in conjunction with these professionals. It employs sage to draw purification and protection, as well as rosemary to cleanse and clear muddied energy.

**Needle and black thread**

**Fashion doll**

**Duct tape**

**Water**

**Container that will accommodate your doll, with a lid**

**Sea salt**

**Herbs: sage, rosemary**

1. Use needle and thread to sew the doll's mouth shut.

2. Place a tiny piece of duct tape over the eyes.

3. Duct tape the hands together, and the feet, as well.

4. Fill your container with water, adding a pinch of sea salt, sage, and rosemary.

5. Place the doll carefully in the container, put the lid on, and set it in your freezer while saying, *I bind your actions; you can't touch me. I bind your words; they can't hurt me. By the power of three, I bind thee. By the power of three, I'm set free.*

6. Leave this in place as long as you need to for peace of mind. If the day comes that you no longer feel this spell is necessary, remove it from the freezer and throw it in the trash in its entirety, container and all.

# The Bogeyman Protection Spell

Even as adults, sometimes we're still afraid of the bogeyman hiding under our bed; put simply, fear is still real no matter our chronological age. But we must learn how to face our fears, and in facing them, realize that we have the power to overcome them. This spell's magical energy will help you do just that, utilizing thyme to encourage a clearer perception of reality, as well as yarrow and St. John's wort to bring courage. Stones represent the four elements in this spell: smoky quartz and moss agate for earth, citrine and yellow calcite for air, garnet and bloodstone for fire, and lapis and blue kunzite for water. Put some thought into your personal effects before performing your magic.

**Large metal, ceramic, or wooden tray**

**4 taper candles: green for earth, yellow for air, red for fire, blue for water**

**4 candle holders**

**4 (or more) stones, with at least 1 from each pair: smoky quartz or moss agate, citrine or yellow calcite, garnet or bloodstone, lapis or blue kunzite**

**Herbs: thyme, yarrow, St. John's wort**

**Incense: sandalwood**

**Incense holder**

**Personal effects, such as a sheet of paper with your fears written out or a physical item representative of your fears, like matches for a fear of fire or a dog collar for fear of dogs**

**Matches**

1. On a large tray on your altar and in an arrangement that is resonant and powerful to you, place the candles representing the four elements in candle holders and *at least one* stone for each element at the base of the candle holders.

2. Sprinkle the herbs on your tray.

3. Place incense and an incense holder on the tray.

4. Finally, add the personal effects representing your fear.

*Continued*

5. When you feel your tray altar is complete, carefully slide it under your bed. From time to time, bring it out to light the candles and incense, to remove something from the tray, or to add new items.

6. You may desire to have an alternate place for your altar, such as a closet or cupboard. As with all altars, you can dismantle this one anytime you feel the desire to do so. However, many practitioners delight in updating their altars from time to time in relation to the seasons or holidays.

# CONCLUSION

Congratulations on finding your way to this magical and inspiring spiritual path. You must have heard the calling to be drawn to this book. Spirit touches those who are destined for this very special way of life. You've learned much through this stage of your journey, and I can tell you that this is only the beginning. Be prepared to spend a lifetime exploring and learning the magic and wonder that encompasses the way of a witch. Read more books, study other sources, and connect with your magical community in whatever way moves you the most.

Through this book, you've met some of the founders of modern Wicca and touched the energy that they've brought to modern paganism. You've learned the empowering holidays that mark the Wiccan year and the Wiccan tools of the trade, as well as how to use them to cast successful spells. You've been given the knowledge to create your own personally charged and meaningful magic.

As you go forward, remember that there is no right way or wrong way to practice the craft—there will only be *your* way. Don't be afraid to explore new ideas and connect with interesting and like-minded people. Keep reading, learning, and practicing. Be strong. Cling to integrity, honesty, empathy, positivity, goodwill, and humbleness as you grow in power and magic.

# RESOURCES

**Blake, Deborah.** *Everyday Witchcraft: Making Time for Spirit in a Too-Busy World.* **St. Paul, MN: Llewellyn Publications, 2015.**
This book teaches you how to incorporate the practice of witchcraft into your life regardless of how busy and hectic that life may be. It's full of wisdom, grace, and humor.

**Chamberlain, Lisa.** *Wicca Candle Magic: A Beginner's Guide to Practicing Wiccan Candle Magic, with Simple Candle Spells.* **Chamberlain Publications, 2015.**
Lisa's book provides the knowledge you need to harness the element of fire through candle magic. She teaches you how to blend other correspondence components with this magic, as well, such as color and spiritual intentions.

**Cunningham, Scott, and David Harrington.** *The Magical Household: Spells & Rituals for the Home.* **St. Paul, MN: Llewellyn Publications, 1987.**
A warm and wise book from a beloved pagan author, this book is full of rites and spells that will help you create a magical household.

**Moura, Ann.** *Green Witchcraft: Folk Magic, Fairy Lore & Herb Craft.* **St. Paul, MN: Llewellyn Publications, 2002.**
This book explores the fundamentals of basic witchcraft from the perspective of the green witch. It provides step-by-step instructions for self-initiation, as well as a variety of magical practices.

**Murphy-Hiscock, Arin.** *The Witch's Book of Self-Care: Magical Ways to Pamper, Soothe, and Care for Your Body and Spirit.* **Avon, MA: Adams Media, 2018.**

This is a self-care book geared to the magical practitioner. It's full of recipes, rituals, and magical spells to pamper the woman in every witch.

**Next Millennium. www.MagicalOmaha.com.**

You can purchase nearly anything magical you need from this shop (which ships worldwide), including stones, herbs, candles, cauldrons, specialty items, ritual clothing, books, tarot cards, and more.

**Nock, Judy Ann.** *The Modern Witchcraft Guide to Magickal Herbs: Your Complete Guide to the Hidden Powers of Herbs.* **Avon, MA: Adams Media, 2019.**

An excellent resource for both the beginner and the experienced practitioner, this book is full of information you need to incorporate herbs successfully in your magical practice.

# SPELL INDEX

# INDEX

# ACKNOWLEDGMENTS

I would like to thank some of the women who have magically inspired me on this decades-long journey through witchcraft: Cordelia, a gentle soul; Shirley, coven sister and kindred spirit; Beverly, soul sister; Cindy, witch extraordinaire and entrepreneur; Suzanne, the ever-cheerful witch at Gray House; and Ms. Julie, creatrix of inspiration. There are so many more, too many to name them all here, but may they all recognize who they are and realize the magic they have spread.

# ABOUT THE AUTHOR

 **Amythyst Raine** is the author of books on witchcraft, the tarot, and Goddess spirituality, including *Green Witchcraft Grimoire*. She creates websites and videos, reads tarot cards, and casts a spell now and then..